A HISTORY (

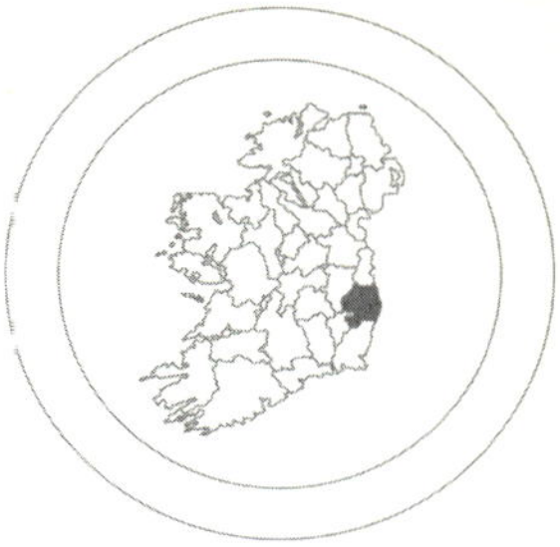

A HISTORY OF COUNTY Wicklow

Arthur Flynn

GILL & MACMILLAN

Gill & Macmillan Ltd
Hume Avenue, Park West, Dublin 12
with associated companies throughout the world
www.gillmacmillan.ie

0 7171 3485 7
Index compiled by Helen Litton
Design by Graham Thew Design
Print origination by Carrigboy Typesetting Services, Co. Cork
Printed by ColourBooks Ltd, Dublin

This book is typeset in 11pt Post-Mediaeval on 14pt.

The paper used in this book comes from the wood pulp of managed forests. For every tree felled, at least one tree is planted, thereby renewing natural resources.

A CIP catalogue record for this book is available from the British Library.

1 3 5 4 2

Cover photographs (*left to right*)
The 12th Earl of Meath c. 1885; Rathdrum Station c. 1890; the bridge at Clara Vale; RIC and British soldiers at Bray Barracks c. 1914; the Round Tower at Glendalough

Dedicated to Geraldine

CONTENTS

ACKNOWLEDGMENTS

I WOULD LIKE TO THANK the following for their assistance in the preparation of this book: the National Library of Ireland, Public Record Office, Trinity College Library, Dáil Library, Tony Roche Dúchas, Wicklow County Council, Jackie Napier, Brian White, Vaughan Dodd, Kathleen Kinsella, Joe Behan, Ernie Gallagher, Henry Cairns, Sean Fox, Jean Costello Coillte, Joan Kavanagh Wicklow Gaol, Lord Meath, Wicklow Tourism, Wicklow Film Commission, George McClafferty and the staff of Glendalough Visitors Centre, GAA, Robert Butler and Noelle Ringwood Ballywaltrim Library, Michael Kelleher and Tom French Bray Library, Dermot de Barra Bray Tourism, and Leah Coyne Wicklow Arts Officer. I would also like to acknowledge the following for the use of photographs: Bord Fáilte, National Library of Ireland, Dúchas, ESB Archives, Rex Roberts Studio, Cambridge University Collection, Alfred Beit Foundation, Hulton-Deutsch Collection, and The Illustrated London News. A special words of thanks to Blaise Treacy, Pat Hunt, Michael Lawlor, Garrett Flynn, Jim Clarke, and Bernie Murphy for reading and advising on the text. My thanks also to the staff of Gill & Macmillan, especially Fergal Tobin and Deirdre Rennison Kunz, for their help and guidance.

I INTRODUCTION

To depict adequately half the delights of beautiful Wicklow would require a large and full volume. We must be content to stimulate the appetite of the tourist so that he may long for the rich banquet which nature has provided for him. Wicklow is indeed the Garden of Ireland; its prominent feature is, indeed, healthful and refreshing sublimity and wild grandeur. But among its high and bleak mountains there are numerous rich and fertile valleys, luxuriantly wooded and with the noblest of magnificent rivers running through them, forming, in their course, a number of cataracts. Its natural graces are enhanced in value because they are invariably encountered after the eye and mind have wearied of gazing upon rude and uncultivated districts covered with peat, upon the scanty herbage on which small sheep can scarcely find pasture. (Samuel Carter Hall and Anna Maria Hall, Ireland: Its Scenery, Character, etc., *1841)*

COUNTY WICKLOW (Contae Chill Mhantáin) is the youngest of the thirty-two counties, having been created in 1606, some four centuries after the original twelve. With a population of 114,719, it covers 500,511 acres (202,552 hectares), or 782 square miles. It extends from the Carlow–Kildare border to a 25-mile coastline on the Irish Sea, from Arklow on the Co. Wexford border in the south to Bray in the north, where it adjoins Co. Dublin. The coastline is varied—from cliffs and isolated coves to long stretches of stony seashore and several sandy beaches, most notably Brittas Bay and the Silver Strand.

Since the late eighteenth century, when the area from Enniskerry to Bray and Delgany became popular with the Anglo-Irish Ascendancy for their country houses and landscaped grounds, Co. Wicklow has been known as the Garden of Ireland. It is a county of contrasts, from the stark mountain passes of the Wicklow Gap and Sally Gap to the towering beauty of Bray Head, the Sugar Loafs, and Lugnaquillia Mountain to the peaks of Kippure and Djouce Mountain. Much of the picturesque landscape was shaped from glacial movement during the Ice Age; the scenic valleys of Glencree, Glenmalure (Glenmalur), Glen of the Downs, Glen of Imail, and Glenmacnass are evidence of this. The arable pastures are confined to the valleys, as there is an extensive covering of blanket bog on the uplands, with the land suitable only for forestry and the rearing of sheep. The central mountainous areas are sparsely populated, and communities are concentrated mainly along the coastal seaboard and the rich pastureland on the western boundaries. The underlying rocks influence plant life, but heather, furze and ferns thrive on the better-drained slopes. While the native red deer are extinct, the offspring of their matings with sika or Japanese deer are still to be found in Co. Wicklow.

Lugnaquillia Mountain, towering 3,035 feet (925 metres) over the Glen of Imail, is the highest peak in the Wicklow Mountains and the second-highest in Ireland, after Carrauntoohil in Co. Kerry, at 3,409 feet (1,039 metres). The long-dormant volcanoes of the Great Sugar Loaf and Little Sugar Loaf are now separated by the N11 road at the Glen of the Downs. From the Rocky Valley the ground rises gradually to Roundwood, which claims the title of highest village in Ireland. North from Roundwood the road rises steeply until it reaches a plateau towering above Lough Tay and Luggala Lodge. The winding mountain road continues through some of Co. Wicklow's most spectacular scenery and highest mountains—Djouce Mountain and War Hill—and on to the Sally Gap crossroads. There are panoramic views from the summit of Bray Head, the Sugar Loafs, and the Motte Stone at Avoca; the Mourne Mountains in Co. Down and the Snowdonia mountains of Wales can be seen on fine days.

The county is laced with rivers and lakes. The Vartry River, which feeds the reservoir at Roundwood, has supplied drinking water to

Dublin for almost 150 years. It enters the sea at Wicklow (where it is known as the Leitrim). The River Liffey rises in Co. Wicklow in a deep pool between Kippure and Tonduff and meanders for 80 miles (130 kilometres) through Cos. Kildare and Dublin before entering the sea in Dublin Bay. The Avonmore and Avonbeg Rivers merge to create the picturesque Meeting of the Waters, immortalised by Thomas Moore in his song of that name. The River Slaney, which enters the sea at Wexford, rises on Lugnaquillia Mountain, while the Dargle River, from its source in Glencree, drains into the sea at Bray. Ireland's highest waterfall, cascading 351 feet (107 metres) into the Dargle Valley at Powerscourt, near Enniskerry, must be one of the most-photographed sights in the country. Glenmacnass, Glenmalure, and Glendasan also possess waterfalls of great beauty.

Megalithic tombs are evidence that the region has been inhabited since the Neolithic Period or Late Stone Age, approximately 4000–2400 BC. Later ring-forts are also visible in the many archaeological sites scattered throughout the county. The numbers of ecclesiastical ruins, small churches, stone crosses, and gravestones throughout the county reveal the impact of Christianity in Ireland. Glendalough and its monastic settlement have been a place of pilgrimage since its foundation in the sixth century and still attract large numbers of visitors. Irish people and visitors alike are attracted by the monastic site and the tranquil beauty of the Upper and Lower Lakes, which combine to make Glendalough one of Ireland's premier attractions.

The lakes at Blessington are unique in Ireland, being artificial. In 1939 the Electricity Supply Board evacuated 44 townlands and flooded 2,600 hectares (6,500 acres) of farms and fields in north-west Co. Wicklow to provide water for the generation of electricity for the rapidly expanding Dublin area. Lough Tay, Lough Bray, and Lough Dan, sheltered by the mountains, are equally scenic but less accessible, best known to the more intrepid tourists and the thousands of hill-walkers who trek the Wicklow Way every year. Scattered throughout the county are miles of unspoilt trails, old coach roads, green roads, pilgrim trails, and bog roads.

The largest towns are Wicklow, the *county town* (administrative capital), Bray and Arklow in the east and Blessington and Baltinglass in the west. There are also the smaller but growing towns of Greystones, Delgany, Enniskerry, and Rathdrum. In the south of the county the main towns and villages are Tinahely, Aughrim, Shillelagh, and Avoca.

The earliest written reference to the area of modern Co. Wicklow is in the works of the second-century Alexandrian astronomer Ptolemy (Claudius Ptolemaeus); his map, though inaccurate, shows a settlement corresponding approximately to present-day Co. Wicklow, with the mouth of a river called Oboka (which was later adopted locally in the form Avoca). We get an early account of the coastal extent of Co. Wicklow in the Norman-French song called 'Dermot and the Earl':

De ridelsford iuint water	*And Walter de Ridelsford came,*
Barun noble guerrer.	*A brave and noble warrior.*
Si li donat wininlo	*He gave him also Wicklow,*
Entre bree e arklo;	*Between Bray and Arklow;*
Co fud la terre de kylmantan	*This was the land of Cill Mhantáin,*
Entre ad cleth e lochgarman.	*Between Áth Cliath and Loch Garman.*

The origins of the English name Wicklow lie in the Norse name *Uíkar-ló*, 'meadow of the bay', the name given by the Vikings to their settlement on the site of the modern town of Wicklow, from which the county is named. Other place-names derived from the Norse are Arklow, Wexford, and Waterford. In the twelfth century, with the arrival of the Anglo-Normans, the name underwent several changes, from *Wygyngalo* to *Wyklow* and finally to *Wicklow*. The Irish name, Cill Mhantáin ('Mantán's chapel'), is supposedly named after one of St Patrick's followers. According to a legend recounted in the Annals of Clonmacnoise in the fifth century, Mantán and Patrick arrived in Wicklow, where a hostile crowd met them and refused them permission to land. Mantán was struck in the face by a rock that knocked all his teeth out, and he became known as Mantán ('gummy'). Some years later he returned to the area and established a monastery there that became known as Cill Mhantáin.

In 1606 Wicklow was declared a county–the last of the thirty-two counties to come officially under the jurisdiction of the English Crown. The shape and scope of the county were predetermined, as all the surrounding counties had previously established their boundaries. Before 1606 Arklow had been in Co. Wexford, Baltinglass had been in Co. Kildare, and Bray and Wicklow had been in Co. Dublin. The west Wicklow towns of Blessington and Baltinglass had more in common with the neighbouring counties of Kildare, Dublin, and Carlow than with their east Wicklow brethren, as the mountain range bisects the county and there were no direct roads linking the county from east to west.

In 1210 the first twelve of the thirty-two counties were 'shired', on the style of the English shires. The Wicklow septs of the O'Byrnes and the O'Tooles would not submit to English rule; the area was declared hostile and so did not become a county until four centuries later. In 1488 the boundaries with Cos. Meath, Louth, and Kildare were defined by an act of Parliament. From the early 1540s a number of attempts were made to 'shire' Co. Wicklow, but to no avail. The first determined attempt was made in 1542 and the last, successful one on 23 September 1603. In 1606 Co. Wicklow was officially declared a county. Up to that year the boundary of Co. Dublin stretched from Gormanston in the north to Arklow in the south, which was then under the control of a sheriff.

In 1578 a royal commission proposed boundaries for Co. Wicklow. The proposal floundered, as there were not enough suitable candidates to serve as sheriffs and freeholders. In 1603 Sir Arthur Chichester (later Lord Deputy of Ireland) proposed that the boundaries set out by the royal commission be accepted. Chichester had been advocating this move for many years. In 1605 Lord Fitzwilliam and Patrick Sarsfield of Lucan surveyed the proposed new shire and accepted the boundaries of the royal commission, with minor modifications. The northern border with Co. Dublin was one such contentious issue.

Finally, in January 1606, Co. Wicklow, consisting of 782 square miles, became the seventeenth-largest of thirty-two counties. It was the responsibility of a King's officer known as the sheriff to regularly assemble twenty-three of the biggest landlords in the county to make up a grand jury, which would decide policies for the new county. Within two centuries Wicklow was transformed from a primarily native Irish region to the most Anglicised of counties. Wicklow County Council has municipal minutes and other records dating from 1663, apart from a gap during the 1798 period, when records were not maintained.

2 ANTIQUITY

The ICE AGE was responsible for shaping much of the geographical appearance of Co. Wicklow. This is most evident in the seven glacial valleys. When the ice began to melt it formed glaciers in the mountains, which left raised granite ridges containing two of the highest passes in the country, the Wicklow Gap and the Sally Gap.

Throughout the mountain ranges melting ice from the glaciers cut 'dry gaps' or deep drainage channels and also formed corry lakes with steep-sided cliffs, as at Lough Bray. Ice also created the Upper and Lower Lakes at Glendalough.

Massive sheets of ice began a gradual shifting, shaping the mountain peaks and scooping out valleys such as Glencree, the Glen of the Downs, the Scalp, and Glenmalure. In the Ice Age a glacial lake existed close to Blessington, stretching approximately 17 miles (28 kilometres) from Brittas in the north to Corragh in the south, about 6 miles (10 kilometres) long and up to 400 feet (120 metres) wide. The ice acted as a dam, trapping the water on the River Liffey and the King's River and creating the huge lake. Shorelines were created as the level dropped, leaving remnants that can be seen at the eastern side of the reservoir, taking the form of step-like features about 3 feet (1 metre) high. Gravel and sand deposited in lakes created deltas that in later years were used for quarrying. The Wicklow Mountains are formed from granite, slate, quartzite, and schist. The county's west-facing glens are broadly granite-based.

At the end of the Ice Age, about nine thousand years ago, the first humans arrived in Ireland, and traces of *Mesolithic* (Middle Stone Age) culture have been found in Co. Wicklow, particularly in the west. In recent excavations along the coast at Brittas Bay small flint-working sites have been discovered. Before the Ice Age the sea level was low, and Ireland was connected to Britain, and Britain to the Continent. The first people possibly crossed from Scandinavia to Britain, then on to Ireland from present-day Scotland, settling mainly on the coast and beside rivers. When the ice melted, the sea level rose, and by 6000 BC Ireland was separated from Britain. As the ice moved northwards, warmer climates facilitated the growth of trees and plant life, and Ireland became blanketed in dense forests.

Stone Age people first arrived on Co. Wicklow's coast more than five thousand years ago. They used simple stone tools for everyday tasks and for hunting. The *Neolithic* (Late Stone Age) culture, approximately 4000–2400 BC, left megalithic tombs in Rathdrum, Brittas, and areas of west Wicklow. At Moylisha, 2 miles (3 kilometres) south of Aghowle church, there is a wedge-shaped gallery grave dating from this period. The massive Motte Stone at Avoca, weighing 100 tonnes, also dates from the Stone Age. Geologists have shown that glaciers swept the stone from rock formations on Lugnaquillia Mountain to the west.

An area of Cambrian rocks laid down during the Palaeolithic era extends from Bray to Wicklow. The south side of Bray Head is a prime example, where green and purple colours show alternating layers of different textures interwoven with grey 'wackies' of sandstone and *quartzite* (sandstone that has been subject to intense heat and pressure). The Bray series of Cambrian rocks is overlaid on Ordovician, possibly laid down some million years previously and among the oldest geological formations in Europe. Some of the oldest fossils in Europe have been found in the vicinity of Bray. More evidence of its ancient past lies in the submerged primaeval forest at the north beach, which has a radiocarbon-dated age of 6,750 years. A dense forest once covered much of the east coast of the county, but through coastal erosion and gradual development it has receded.

Forests have always featured in the landscape of Co. Wicklow, and the early settlers found the land covered in dense woodlands of pine and hazel. On higher ground in the Wicklow Mountains there were primarily dense pine forests, inhabited by wolves, giant deer, and bears, which has been confirmed by discoveries in bog excavations. The density of the woodlands appears to have confined settlements to coastal areas.

A particularly good forest in Glencree was chosen in 1224 as the 'royal forest', and eighty deer were sent from Chester to stock the 'King's Park' at Glencree. Shillelagh was noted for its oak woods, and a representative of the Crown reported that 'the woods of Shillelagh are sufficient for the King's ships for twenty years.' In the seventeenth century forests became an important source of revenue in the export of timber and of fuel for mining and iron-smelting.

The BRONZE AGE

The people of the Bronze Age (approximately 2400 BC to AD 600) were to leave traces of mine-workings, cuttings, and ancillary buildings, and burial places. Bronze, the first metal to be worked extensively, is a mixture of copper and tin and was shaped to manufacture tools and weapons. Co. Wicklow has always been an important source of minerals. The Annals of the Four Masters stated that gold was smelted in the kingdom of Cualann, and there is evidence that gold was worked there since the Bronze Age. The passage tomb at Parknasilloge and that at Onagh, close to Enniskerry, are strong evidence that the area was inhabited during the Bronze Age.

Old roads, stone forts, promontory forts, and earthen ring-forts dating from about 1500 BC can be seen in the Baltinglass area. This area of west Wicklow is particularly rich in archaeological finds from the Late Bronze Age (approximately 1300–600 BC). Large hilltop enclosures are to be found at Rathcoran and Rathnagree on the 383-metre (1,258-foot) Baltinglass Hill. One of the most extensive hill-forts, that at Rathgall on the Wicklow–Carlow border, dates from the Late Bronze Age and reveals evidence of a circular settlement within fortifications. In further excavations at Baltinglass Hill archaeologists discovered the remains of a passage tomb and five burial chambers dating from the Bronze Age. On Church Mountain, above Donard, there is another chambered cairn.

In recent decades there have been a number of important archaeological finds in this locality. An *ogham* stone (bearing a primitive version of the alphabet, comprising a series of notches cut into the edge) was found here. Also discovered were a number of stone circles, around which people may have celebrated the festival of Lúnasa (the end of summer). In the townland of Carrig, close to Blessington, a cairn was discovered during excavations in 1984. In recent road works at Ashford a significant Bronze Age settlement, consisting of eighteen burnt mounds, was excavated, giving credence to the belief that Bronze Age people manufactured gold jewellery in this area. Human remains from this period were also discovered. In a recent archaeological excavation at Kilmacanogue a round house dating from approximately 1500 BC was unearthed.

Throughout north Co. Wicklow other ring-fort habitations have been unearthed, suggesting the existence of large localised communities. In 2000 the Heritage Service ordered excavations to be carried out on the proposed site of a new golf club on the western slope of Bray Head. These unearthed artefacts dating from the Bronze Age.

The IRON AGE

A ring-fort at Delgany has been dated to the Iron Age (approximately 600 BC to AD 500). There is a *crannóg* (lake dwelling) at Annamoe that also dates from this period. Close to Hollywood, at Athgreany, there is a circle of sixteen granite boulders known as the Piper's Stone. Some of the stones are up to 6 feet (2 metres) high, and the area is about 72 feet (22 metres) wide. Co. Wicklow is rich in ancient sites and relics of the prehistoric, pre-Christian and Christian eras, including passage tombs, ring-forts, raths, and cairns. At Seefin, off the Sally Gap road, there are a number of passage tombs dating from the Early Christian era.

While it is acknowledged that the Romans never invaded Ireland, there is evidence that some Romans landed at Bray. This was confirmed in 1835 when workmen digging a foundation on the beach near the base of Bray Head discovered skeletons lying side by side in graves. A remarkable aspect of the find was Roman copper coins resting on the breast of each body. There is speculation that they were the crew of a

Roman galley that had been wrecked nearby and that survivors had performed the funeral rituals.

The barony of Rathdown, on the southern slopes of Bray Head, was the reputed stronghold of one of Ireland's earliest legendary kings, Eireamhón. This area is rich in historical significance. It is the site of the thirteenth-century Rathdown Castle and also of St Crispen's Church. In recent excavations the Rathdown Hoard, comprising Irish and Spanish coins dating from the sixteenth and seventeenth centuries, was discovered in the area.

3 The CHRISTIAN ERA

CHRISTIANITY CAME to Ireland in the fifth century. Co. Wicklow contributed in no small way to the Christianisation of the country, as is evident from its connections with Sts Kevin and Laurence O'Toole, as well as its reputed connections with Palladius and Patrick. Many of Co. Wicklow's ancient churches, monasteries, inscribed crosses, round towers, and holy wells date from the Early Christian period. Close to some of the early religious sites are 'bullauns' or large stones with a sunken area, believed to have been used for crushing grain.

PALLADIUS

In 431 Pope Celestine sent a bishop named Palladius and his companions Sylvester, Solinus, Augustine, and Benedict to Ireland to establish Christianity and to build churches. Palladius's landing place is not known, but tradition has it that he attempted to come ashore at Arklow, where he received a hostile reception from a local chief, Naithí Mac Garrchoin. Undeterred, he moved up the coast and landed at Wicklow, and it was in this vicinity that he reputedly made his first converts and set up three churches. He built a church at Tigroney, close to Avoca, said to be the first Christian church built in Ireland. It is believed that he built another church at Cillín Chormaic, close to Dunlavin. The cairn on top of Church Mountain marks the site of another church associated with Palladius. There is strong belief that when Palladius arrived in the region the number of his converts increased so rapidly that they built three churches near Donard to accommodate the congregations. Two of Palladius's companions, Sylvester and Salonius, were buried close to one of these churches, that of Donard. It is believed that their bodies were removed to Dunganstown when the Vikings attacked the area.

Palladius felt that his visit had not been successful, and he went to Rome, but he died on the homeward journey.

PATRICK

Many Irish raiding parties crossed the Irish Sea to plunder coastal towns and settlements on the west coast of Britain. During one such raid, probably in the middle of the fifth century, sixteen-year-old Patricius, son of a Roman-British official named Calpurnius, was kidnapped and taken back to Ireland. For the next six years he was set tending sheep, but he turned his attention to God. He eventually escaped and returned home to his family. He later joined the priesthood, and then requested the Pope to send him back to Ireland to continue his mission, as in his dreams he had heard the Irish people calling him. According to legend he landed in Arklow, where St Patrick's Well at Arklow Rock reputedly sprang up when he stepped ashore, but he was also rejected by Naithí Mac Garrchoin and was forced to return to his boat.

According to legend, the Mantán after whom the town of Wicklow is named was one of Patrick's companions, who established a monastery in the area. Two churches in the environs of Avoca, at Kilmagig and Kilpatrick, were once believed to have been founded by St Patrick. The village of Kiltegan (Cill Téagáin) in west Wicklow takes its name from Téagán, a follower of St Patrick, while Rathnew is associated with the saint Earnán Mac Creisine.

During the sixth century there was frequent warfare among the Irish chieftains, mainly over territory. One such chieftain was the king of Leinster, Bran Dubh, who lived in the townland of Rathbran, near Grangecon, in west Wicklow. In 598 there was a battle at Dún Bolg in which the force of Bran Dubh killed the king of Uí Néill, Ard Mac Ainmhirigh. Such was the slaughter that it is said that years of famine followed.

The Irish chiefs and septs (clan or tribe) were at first suspicious of Christianity but slowly began to accept the preaching of the monks. About this time another early monastic settlement was established at Aghowl, west of Shillelagh. This settlement was founded by St Finnéan of Clonard, Co. Westmeath. Only a small church built on the site in the twelfth century remains today.

KEVIN

It was against this background that Christianity obtained a foothold in Ireland. One of the most important sites from the sixth century onwards was Glendalough (Gleann Dá Loch, 'valley of the two lakes'), famous for its Early Christian monastery, founded by Kevin (Anglicised name of Caoimhín), combined with the great scenic beauty of the surroundings. Caoimhín was reputedly born in 498 in west Wicklow and entered a monastery, where he was ordained a priest. Anxious to be alone to pray and meditate, he moved first to Hollywood and later to Glendalough, where he lived as a hermit in a cell above the Upper Lake now known as St Kevin's Bed. He observed a life of prayer, fasting and penance for a considerable time. Nobody was aware of his presence until a shepherd discovered Caoimhín among his herd of cows. The shepherd told his friends, and people came to see the holy man. They were curious at first but gradually began to join him in prayer.

According to tradition, in 570 Caoimhín was appointed first abbot of Glendalough and founded a monastery there. One by one, over a two-mile radius, rose the seven churches of Glendalough. There are many legends about the saint. One relates that when women carrying baskets of cheese refused to give him any he turned the cheese into stones. By the time of his death in 618 Glendalough had become established as a place of learning and spirituality; its reputation was to spread throughout Europe, and many scholars travelled there from abroad. The monks studied the works of Latin classical writers and began copying brilliantly illustrated Irish manuscripts. In 639 St Dagán, according to tradition a nephew of St Patrick, lived in a cell at Ennereilly, north of Arklow, and later founded a monastery there.

St Kevin's Way, a pilgrim path on which the saint is reputed to have travelled from Hollywood to Glendalough, has recently been reopened. The trail begins at St Kevin's Well in Hollywood and follows the route through Hollywood Glen to Dunboyke, site of an early church dedicated to the saint. It then climbs steeply to the Wicklow Gap, past Lough Nahanagan, dipping alongside the Glendasan River to the monastic settlement at Glendalough. There are many other pilgrimage trails and roads scattered throughout the county.

The VIKINGS

From 795, Norse raiders known as Vikings or *Ostmen* (men of the east) launched raids on the east coast of Ireland. The first base they established was at the ford of the Liffey, present-day Dublin. From here they fanned out and set up other fortifications on estuaries, from which they were able to plunder the countryside. Monasteries were one of their principal targets. They quickly realised that the richest monasteries were inland; but the rivers were like highways to the Viking longships, which, with their shallow draught, could penetrate far inland. They would secure a river by establishing a base at its mouth, which they could defend with a wall and rough fortifications. They chose several obvious places along the east coast: Bray, at the mouth of the Dargle, Wicklow, at the estuary of the Vartry, and Arklow, at the mouth of the Avoca. Wicklow and Arklow were originally established as trading centres but later became more extensive settlements.

In Wicklow the Vikings established themselves on a promontory called the Round Mound. Soon they were influential enough to give names to some areas. The Broad Lough became known as Wiggingle Lought ('lake of the ships'), referring to the lakes behind the Murrough, which provided a safe haven for their ships. They built a fortification on the rock that later became known as the Black Castle. This bastion was strategically placed over the Vartry River, giving the Vikings control of the estuary.

For centuries an area along the Vartry River was known as the Vineyard Banks. According to local folklore the Vikings planted these vines. A clover native to the Mediterranean that grows on the Murrough is also credited to the Vikings, being reputed to have come in the ballast of their longships.

The area around Bray was handed over to the Torkjell family, whose domain extended from Donnybrook to Glencree. In Viking times the land lying between Bray and Dublin was called Dubh-Ghall ('land of the dark foreigners'), after the Danes, to differentiate it from Fingall (Fionn-Ghall, 'land of the fair foreigners'), on the north side of Dublin. From 795 the Vikings realised what wealth lay in golden chalices and illustrated manuscripts in monasteries. There was little security around the isolated, vulnerable monasteries, and they were easy targets. From their base in Arklow they staged ruthless attacks on the monasteries at Glendalough, Kildare and Ferns and plundered and burned them on a number of occasions. It was formerly believed that Ireland's famous round towers, such as that at Glendalough, were used as refuges during such raids; these are in fact bell towers, and would not have been efficient places of refuge. Following these attacks, many of the Vikings returned to Scandinavia with their loot.

LAURENCE O'TOOLE

By the beginning of the ninth century the ecclesiastical city that had developed from the monastery at Glendalough had risen to a position of wealth. At its head was the abbot, who often nominated his own successor. In 1111, following the Synod of Ráth Bhreasail, Glendalough was designated one of the two sees of north Leinster. Another saint to have a long association with Wicklow was Laurence O'Toole (Anglicised name of Lorcán Ó Tuathail). He was born in 1128, son of Muircheartach Ó Tuathail, king of the Uí Muirí dynasty of north Leinster. His sister was married to Diarmaid Mac Murchú (known today as Dermot MacMurrough), king of Leinster, who was opposed to the young Ó Tuathail. MacMurrough made war on Lorcán's father and forced him to hand over his son as a hostage as part of their settlement. Lorcán's father reputedly captured twelve of MacMurrough's men and threatened to kill them if the boy was not released.

Lorcán was twelve years old when MacMurrough handed him over to the Bishop of Glendalough. Muircheartach went to thank the bishop and, as was then the custom, offered to give one of his sons to the church. Young Lorcán offered himself, and he was allowed to join the priesthood. He was ordained, and he showed such determination that he became abbot of Glendalough at the age of twenty-five. In 1161 he was appointed archbishop of Dublin, but he repeatedly returned to the solitude of St Kevin's Bed. Seventeen years later the Pope appointed him Papal Legate to Ireland. When Ruairí Ó Conchúir, the High King, insulted King Henry II of England, Lorcán was sent to Normandy, where Henry lived, to bring about reconciliation between them. There he contracted a fever, from which he died in 1180, and he was buried in Normandy. He is believed to have been canonised in 1226 by Pope Honorius.

In 1148 Dermot MacMurrough, king of Leinster, built a monastery for the Cistercians at Baltinglass, Co. Wicklow, and endowed them with eight separate grants of land. The abbey, known as Vallis Salutis ('valley of health'), was one of the first to be occupied by the order, which had arrived in Ireland six years previously. The politics of the period demanded such a contribution from local kings and chieftains. In 1397 the Irish Parliament sat in the abbey for three days. In later years the monks were accused of sheltering rebels, and were harassed.

GLENDALOUGH

The Vatican was impressed by the development of the religious centre at Glendalough and encouraged its progress by issuing two 'bulls' or proclamations concerning it. In 1179 it was mentioned in a bull of Pope Alexander III in which he took the diocese of Glendalough under his control and confirmed its possessions on Bishop Malchus. In 1198 Pope Innocent III also referred to Glendalough in a Papal bull. In 1267 Glendalough was created an independent parish, the incumbent being a canon of St Patrick's Cathedral, Dublin. In modern times the ruins of the churches have been partially restored. Despite being the county's leading tourist attraction, Glendalough remains a place of peace and tranquillity.

From their coastal settlements at the estuaries of the Dargle, Vartry, and Avoca Rivers the Vikings repeatedly raided monasteries such as those at Glendalough. As they murdered the monks and looted their monasteries they engaged in warfare with the Irish septs. In their strongholds on the east coast they were protected from the powerful Leinster tribes and could also stage random attacks on English coastal towns.

The name Arklow is of Norse origin. At the time of the Viking invasions the settlement here, known to the Irish as An tInbhear Mór ('the great estuary'), had connections with Aimheirghin, son of the legendary Míle. It subsequently became known as *Arnkell-ló* ('Arnkell's meadow'), after a Norse chieftain who took over this area. One road in the town is now called Danes' Road.

In 1214 King John of England renewed his grant to the then Archbishop of Dublin, when it was planned to place Glendalough under the archbishopric. The O'Tooles treated his grant with contempt, and the forces of the Crown attacked Glendalough. In 1250, following numerous attacks and considerable damage to the monastery of Glendalough, Maurice Fitzgerald, Baron of Naas, saw the need for a replacement, and he founded a monastery for the Franciscan Minors in the town of Wicklow. It came under the patronage of the O'Byrnes, a move that protected it during many years of war and unrest. After the dissolution of the monasteries the building was used as a court-house. The Franciscans also founded a monastery in Arklow at about this time. Later, David Wolfe established the Maudelin Leper House in Wicklow.

In contrast to the hostility of the Vikings, the Anglo-Normans gave patronage to religious practices, and many of the invaders intermarried with the Irish. In the twelfth century the Normans encouraged religious orders to establish monasteries and abbeys in Ireland: the Franciscans, Augustinians, Dominicans, and Carmelites all responded to the invitation and founded churches and monasteries.

4 The MIDDLE AGES

IN THE EARLY twelfth century the territory of the O'Tooles was known as Uí Muirí and Uí Máil. This extended southwards from Powerscourt to Castledermot and westward from Glendalough to Athy. The O'Tooles were then under the dominance of Dermot MacMurrough, who had become chief of his sept at the age of sixteen and brought the O'Tooles under his control when he became king of Leinster. Many of the other Leinster septs were in dispute with MacMurrough and sought every opportunity to undermine him.

The Anglo-Norman invasion began as a result of a personal vendetta between Dermot MacMurrough and Tiarnán Ó Ruairc of Bréifne. In 1152 MacMurrough abducted Ó Ruairc's wife and held her hostage for a year. It was 1166 before Ó Ruairc found an opportunity for revenge, when he secured the help of MacMurrough's enemies among the other Leinster septs and successfully attacked his base in Ferns and banished him. MacMurrough, realising that his kingship and territory were in danger, turned for support to friends in Wales. Within the tribal system of the time the Welsh were nearer and more in touch with Leinster than the septs of the other provinces of Ireland. MacMurrough requested assistance from King Henry II of England in reclaiming his lands.

Pope Adrian IV (the Englishman Nicholas Breakspear) had previously expressed concern about the role of the Church in Ireland. Henry II had discussions with him about the possibility of a reforming crusade in Ireland, and he received the Pope's blessing to take whatever action he considered necessary. MacMurrough's appeal provided him with the ideal opportunity to justify acting on the Pope's edict. With Henry's authority, MacMurrough travelled through England and Wales gathering a force. Richard fitz Gilbert de Clare, better known as Strongbow, agreed to assist him in the invasion, but on a number of conditions. Strongbow was ambitious and sought to become king of Leinster following the death of MacMurrough. He also asked for MacMurrough's eldest daughter, Aoife, as his wife. Reluctantly, MacMurrough agreed to these terms and so opened the way for the first Anglo-Norman invasion—the beginning of the rule of the English Crown in Ireland.

In 1167 MacMurrough arrived back in Ireland, landing at Bannow Bay, Co. Wexford, with a small force of Anglo-Norman mercenaries. In May and August 1169 and August 1170 further groups of Anglo-Norman knights and mercenaries arrived, among them Strongbow, who attacked and seized the town of Waterford. These were experienced soldiers who realised that they needed to secure the principal port of the east coast if they were to gain maximum control, and so they set out to take Dublin. The High King, Ruairí Ó Conchúir, anticipated this move and established defences on the main approach roads. He was confident that he could block their advance in the ravine at the Scalp and at Windgates near Bray; but he had not reckoned on the wily MacMurrough and his knowledge of the countryside. Like Hannibal leading his elephants across the Alps, he led the invaders across the mountains through the passes at Glendalough and Glencree, avoiding the waiting Irish forces. They proceeded to the walls of Dublin, and within days it had fallen to MacMurrough and his allies.

The Anglo-Norman adventurers appreciated the importance of the ports and seashore of the east coast, and they secured and occupied the entire coastline from Bray to Wicklow and some distance inland in the name of the King of England. Henry II granted most of Leinster to Strongbow but retained the narrow coastal strip from Dublin to Arklow under his own control. The invaders quickly established settlements at Bray, Wicklow, Newcastle, and Arklow, where they built defensive castles. In the early period of the Anglo-Norman conquest they erected a distinctive style of fortification known as a motte and bailey. These were mounds of earth up to 30 feet (10 metres) high, with steep sides; a wooden structure was then built on top of the mound for defence and also as living quarters. A wooden bridge connected the motte to the bailey or lower area. If the inhabitants came under attack they could withdraw the bridge and keep their attackers at bay.

The BLACK CASTLE

In 1171 Dermot MacMurrough died, and Strongbow was crowned king of Leinster, but he encountered strong opposition from the Irish septs. Henry II, feeling uneasy with Strongbow's grasp of power and fearing that he could be a threat to his own supremacy, arrived in Ireland with a large force. Landing in Co. Waterford, he marched north, and the Irish septs submitted to him. He shared out areas of the conquered land among his knights. Maurice Fitzgerald, ancestor of the Earls of Wicklow, was granted much of the area that was later to become Co. Wicklow. The Fitzgeralds built the Black Castle on the site of an earlier Viking settlement, on the rocky outcrop overlooking the harbour at Wicklow. The Vikings were astute in choosing sites for their settlements, and Fitzgerald was wise to follow their example. There was a safe harbour large enough to accommodate many ships, with a promontory for a look-out position. This site proved to be a good bulwark against attack, easily defensible on the landward side and with good visibility out to sea, and it withstood many attempted assaults. Sections of this castle still stand today, although in ruins. In 1176 Maurice Fitzgerald died, and his sons were dispossessed of their inheritance by William fitz Aldelm and exiled to Ferns, Co. Wexford.

The settlement that grew to surround the Black Castle gradually developed to become the town of Wicklow, whose name was later adopted for the county. Such was the importance of the settlement at the castle that the area was later granted a royal charter by King James I of England and another by King James II. The town evolved to become the administrative centre of the district, and it is now the seat of local government. A *portreeve* (ruler or mayor) was appointed to encourage freemen and merchants to establish their trades in the new corporate town. From among their ranks, burgesses emerged to represent the citizenry. The Normans were to bring a mediaeval European dimension to the social and economic life of the district, while guilds, established to promote trade, became an influential force in local government.

DE RIDELSFORD

Another significant town was to develop in a similar manner when, in 1172, the lands of Arklow were granted to Theobald Walter, who later became 'Chief Butler of Ireland'. He built a castle, which for a time was the seat of the Earls of Ormonde.

Strongbow also allocated lands among his own Norman followers. Walter de Ridelsford received lands in Cos. Wicklow, Dublin, and Kildare as a reward for killing the Viking known as John the Mad, who was attempting to kill the Governor of Dublin, Milo de Cogan. De Ridelsford married Amabilia, daughter of Henry fitz Henry, a son of King Henry I, and he built the great castle of Bré (Bray) as a well-fortified outpost overlooking the Dargle River to protect the valuable lands south of Dublin. This fortress came under attack many times from the O'Byrnes and the O'Tooles.

Several smaller castles were built in the vicinity, at Fassaroe, Old Connaught, Little Bray, and Oldcourt; with their small garrisons these proved to be easier targets for the attacking Irish. Villages sprang up around these fortifications, and in time they were granted markets. In 1213, when Walter de Ridelsford died, his son, also Walter, succeeded him.

ROYAL CASTLES

In this period there were only two royal castles in Ireland, one in Dublin and the other in Newcastle, Co. Wicklow. This was the castle built there as the King's Manor by Hugh de Lacy, governor of Ireland from 1177 to 1184, on lands confiscated from the O'Tooles (Uí Tuathail), who had opposed the Anglo-Norman invasion. They retreated into the Wicklow Mountains to join forces with the other septs that had been uprooted and dispossessed of their lands in Co. Kildare. The original 'New Castle' was a wooden structure, but it was rebuilt in stone by King Edward I. In the thirteenth century the Manor of Bray was included in possessions assigned to the Crown by de Ridelsford's descendant Christina de Marisco. Previously the manor had been granted to Sir Theobald Butler, an ancestor of the Butlers of Ormonde, in return for the services of an armed horseman to be sent when required to the gates of Dublin Castle to relay messages.

In 1213 King John declared the area a borough, one of several hundred created in Ireland at that time. De Ridelsford was granted a licence to hold a weekly market on Thursdays. The principal tenants in the Manor of Bray were the Knights Templars and the Vicar of Bray. Among the merchants plying their trade in the town there is a record of a successful milling business adjoining the castle operated by Robert the Baker.

In the decade following the Anglo-Norman invasion, confiscated Irish lands were granted to Norman knights and adventurers. In 1225 Walter de Bendevill was granted land at Delgany, where he built Kindlestown Castle. In 1260 Geoffrey de Marisco was granted tracts of land at Hollywood and Donard. Being deprived of their holdings, the Irish septs retreated into the mountains, where they regrouped and remained untouchable. Despite the arrival of reinforcements and the best efforts of the English, these septs could not be defeated. The two most prominent in the history of Co. Wicklow were the O'Byrnes and the O'Tooles, who had originally inhabited lands in Co. Kildare. These septs reigned supreme in their mountain settlements and were responsible for the continued state of war between the native Irish and the Anglo-Norman and later English government in Dublin. The O'Byrnes and the O'Tooles frequently engaged in joint military operations by attacking and destroying the coastal castles of the Normans before retreating to their strongholds. In 1310 they launched one of their most successful attacks and destroyed the Castle of Bré.

In 1315 Edward Bruce, brother of Robert Bruce, king of Scotland, landed in Ireland and declared himself king of Ireland. At the time of the Bruce invasion the castles of Bray, Arklow, and Newcastle had been burned, and the lands around them lay waste for many years. In Bray a fortress was constructed in granite from the ruins of de Ridelsford's castle, and Geoffrey Crump was given a lease of the property. A militia force was raised from the garrison at Bray by a levy on landowners between Bray and Dublin. This force proved to be ineffective and was replaced by mounted men at arms, twenty light horsemen and forty archers under the command of Sir John de Bermingham. In 1316 the O'Byrnes and O'Tooles attacked Arklow and burned many buildings but were defeated by Edward Bruce, who was killed in 1318 at the Battle of Faughart in Co. Louth.

By the early fourteenth century many of the castles had been rebuilt in granite and offered stronger resistance to repeated attacks. The castle at Bray was one of the most important garrison posts, as it protected the ford on the Dargle River on the main route along the east coast. Other castles at Castlekevin, Delgany, Newcastle, Wicklow, and Arklow also had strong garrisons. Smaller castles were built throughout the county to withstand attacks by the Irish septs. The coastal fortresses were relatively safe from attack, but inland settlers were more vulnerable.

The Anglo-Norman landlords developed villages and communities around their castles and manors. Forests were cleared, and small industries and trades were established. Permits were granted for the holding of markets and fairs, with trinkets and leatherwork hawked on the street alongside fish, vegetables, and other foodstuffs. Troubadours, actors, jugglers, and all kinds of street entertainers mingled with mendicants seeking alms from the relatively affluent inhabitants. Many of the Norman settlers adapted easily to the Irish way of life. They married Irish women and began to adopt Irish customs in dress and language, and within a generation some had become 'more Irish than the Irish themselves.'

The Viceroy, Piers Gaveston, opened a pass linking his stronghold at Castlekevin, near Roundwood, with Glendalough, using his power to overrule the objections of the Irish inhabitants. Many expeditions were launched from the castle in an attempt to flush out the O'Tooles and the O'Byrnes. Some of the O'Tooles were bought over and made a deal with the authorities, and they were allowed to function openly in the district, in exchange for labouring under the sheriff of Newcastle and paying taxes and tithes. Dáithí Mac Giolla Chomhaill Ó Tuathail refused to pay his rent and taxes to his overlords and had to vacate his lands. In 1307 the Justiciar, John de Wogan, granted Glenealy, which had been held by the O'Tooles, to the O'Byrnes. This was a deliberate policy by the English to divide the Irish, making them easier to subjugate.

At this time England was engaged in wars in Scotland and France, and its resources were stretched on three fronts. In 1315 King Edward II withdrew much of his army and barons from the area for an invasion of Scotland. The Kilcoole branch of the O'Tooles took advantage of the situation and attacked the timber convoys and burned the castles. The Earls of Ormonde withstood many attacks on their stronghold of Arklow Castle, but in 1331 the Irish succeeded in taking it. The following year the Lord Justice, Anthony de Lucey, recaptured the castle and returned it to the Butlers, who rebuilt it with more impregnable fortifications.

During the fourteenth century the English government, fearing an Irish revival, made funds available for mounting expeditions to control and suppress the 'rebel' septs. These sporadic expeditions proved expensive and, in the main, unsuccessful. A Dublin annalist gave the following description of a campaign in 1329:

> *Sir John Darcy, Justiciar of Ireland, went to the area of Newcastle McKynegan and Wicklow against the O'Byrnes; and . . . the more notable of the Irish were killed, many were wounded, and the remainder fled. And Murrough O'Byrne gave himself up as a hostage together with his son, his uncle, and his uncle's son. But afterwards they were released in return for other hostages, that is, for the more important members of their kin.*

During this period, economic development was stunted by the frequent outbreak of plagues. One of the most devastating was the European pandemic of bubonic and pneumonic plague known as the Black Death. The Norman and Irish inhabitants of the Pale were to suffer most, with thousands of deaths resulting. The birth rate also fell, and many trades ceased completely.

In 1360 the Earl of Stafford, heading a large army, sailed from Liverpool in a campaign against the Irish of Co. Wicklow, but the expedition was aborted when his force was diverted to France on the orders of the King.

KING RICHARD II

In 1394 King Richard II came to Ireland at the head of a large army in another attempt to bring the septs of Leinster under his control. His main objective was to subdue the king of Leinster, Art MacMurrough Caomhánach. At first Art opposed and attacked the forces of the Crown, but, faced with the overpowering force of weaponry and men, he submitted. Richard succeeded in getting submissions and commitments from Art and about seventy other chiefs that they would not attack the forces or property of the Crown. The majority of the O'Tooles and O'Byrnes were more resilient opponents and remained resolute in their independence.

Such was Richard's determination to rule in Ireland that he returned five years later with a stronger army in an effort to finally defeat the remainder of the recalcitrant Wicklow septs. He burned and plundered Glendalough, and the monastery and churches were laid to ruin. While Richard was in Leinster, his enemy Henry Bolingbroke of Lancaster was mustering forces to replace him. When Bolingbroke seized the English throne as King Henry IV, Richard abruptly abandoned his expedition in Ireland and returned to England. But he was forced to abdicate, and he died the following year in prison. During the Middle Ages no other monarch was to come in person to Ireland to declare supremacy.

The new King of England, Henry IV, was more successful in securing the grip of the English Crown on Ireland. An early success in his reign occurred in 1402, when a fierce battle was fought on the outskirts of Bray, in which the septs and citizens of Dublin, headed by the Lord Mayor, John Drake, defeated a force of the O'Byrnes. The battlefield, where more than four hundred people were killed, became known as Bloody Bank (now Sunnybank). To commemorate the victory, the Corporation of Dublin received the privilege of walking behind a gilt sword in procession.

The WAR OF The ROSES

From 1447, England was further weakened by the struggle for the throne between Lancastrian and Yorkist factions known as the War of the Roses, which lasted for thirty years. In 1449 King Richard III replaced the weak Henry VI as monarch. Ireland was to become an important factor in this new regime, mainly because of the English colony's espousal of the Yorkist cause. In 1461 the Yorkists were victorious, and Edward IV was crowned king.

In 1485 King Richard III was killed by followers of Henry Tudor at the Battle of Bosworth. He was succeeded by King Henry VII, and the Tudors became more involved in Irish affairs. Henry allowed Gerald Fitzgerald, Earl of Kildare, to continue as Lord Deputy. While the situation in Ireland could not be completely ignored, England's involvement in a war against France left its coffers depleted. Ireland was a troublesome colony, where even areas of the Pale were constantly under attack by the Irish. The Crown was often restricted in sending reinforcements to relieve its beleaguered supporters.

By the end of the fifteenth century Ireland was primarily ruled by chieftains who offered a nominal allegiance to England. Norman and English knights in Co. Wicklow were in the main responsible for the economic development of the county; they invested in the erection of many castles, keeps, and big houses, including Powerscourt House, near Enniskerry (by the Wingfields, Earls of Powerscourt), and Kilruddery House, near Bray (by the Brabazons, Earls of Meath), monuments to the social standing of the owners. Other prominent but less opulent tower-houses were erected at Burgage and at Three Castles, both in the Kilbride area. These rectangular stone houses, though plain in appearance, were impressive, being four storeys high. The Anglo-Norman and English aristocracy also invested in the infrastructure of the locality, though for their own benefit. They commissioned the building of entire villages for their estate workers and tenants, and some of Co. Wicklow's villages still show evidence of their origin as estate villages, such as Dunlavin, Blessington, and Stratford.

For the next three centuries the Wicklow Mountains were to remain the impenetrable stronghold of the O'Tooles and the O'Byrnes and from where they continued to launch raids on the fortifications of Co. Wicklow. They were joined by other septs that had been dispossessed of their lands in Co. Kildare and had also taken refuge in the Wicklow Mountains. In these hit-and-run raids they destroyed property and seized livestock before retreating into the dense woodlands, where it was impossible for their pursuers to detect them.

The PALE

In 1494 King Henry sent a new Viceroy, Sir Edward Poynings, to Ireland. Poynings, an able officer and administrator, summoned a Parliament at Drogheda, at which he introduced legislation that would reduce the whole country to obedience. Under Poynings' Law the Irish Parliament could assemble only at the behest of the King of England, and any new legislation had to be approved by him. Any Irish chief who acted independently was to be charged with treason.

Such a fate was to befall the Earl of Kildare, Gerald (Gearóid Mór) Fitzgerald.

Poynings designated an area on the east coast around Dublin that would be completely loyal to the Crown. This area, which became known as the English Pale, consisted of the lowland regions of Cos. Dublin, Meath, Louth, and Kildare and at times some of north Wicklow, and it was surrounded by a double ditch. The English within the Pale had to be prepared for frequent and unexpected raids, and a regular garrison, consisting of 1,100 men, was maintained in Bray. This garrison often had to fight to protect not only the town but also this important approach road to Dublin. At the end of the fifteenth century the Pale stretched from Dundalk in the north to Dalkey in the south and westwards to Naas.

The O'Byrne sept quarrelled among themselves and divided into two groups, and each branch dealt with this new threat in a different way. The senior branch, which had become Anglicised and was amenable to keeping within the law in return for a limited amount of freedom, controlled the territory known as Críoch Bhranach, extending from Delgany to Arklow and covering the greater part of east Co. Wicklow. The other group, Gabhal Raghnaill, lived in the area between Rathdrum and Shillelagh and continued to resist English rule; they joined with the O'Tooles and Kavanaghs in raiding English settlements and imposing 'black rents' on them, a form of forced payment to ensure protection from attack on person and property.

Not everyone was as antagonistic as the Wicklow septs. Many were drawn to live in the Pale, lured by its relative peace and stability. Some towns within the Pale were overcrowded, and epidemics of cholera, smallpox, and typhoid were common as a result of the cramped and unsanitary living conditions.

KING HENRY VIII

In 1509 Henry VIII, son of the Tudor King Henry VII, succeeded to the throne of England. He was to pursue a more vigorous policy not only towards the native Irish but also towards the English barons in Ireland who were partial towards the Irish chiefs. In 1533 Henry sought a divorce from his wife, Katherine of Aragon, but the Pope refused him permission. Following his marriage to Anne Boleyn he broke with Rome and rejected the authority of the Pope. This precipitated the English Reformation, by which the King became the 'only Supreme Head on Earth of the whole Church of Ireland.' In 1541 the Irish Parliament declared Henry VIII king of Ireland. Immediately he announced that the complete Anglicisation of the country was necessary. He mounted a strong challenge to Irish culture by demanding a uniform adoption of English dress, language, and laws, and he sent loyal English Protestants to colonise Ireland. Thus began the period of the 'Protestant Ascendancy'. This policy was to cause much religious and political strife in Ireland.

Henry instructed the Viceroy, Gerald (Gearóid Óg) Fitzgerald, ninth Earl of Kildare, to attack the O'Tooles in the Glen of Imail. Fitzgerald forced his way into the glen and killed one of their chiefs, Seán Ó Tuathail, in his bed and sent his head to Henry, who had it placed on a spike on London Bridge. Fitzgerald made another foray into the glen but was ambushed in Hollywood Glen by Seán Óg Ó Tuathail, who wiped out the entire force.

Under Henry the Pale remained a politically distinct region, and in 1536 he extended its boundary to the south of Bray. He established the Talbot family in the lands and castle of Rathdown, north of Greystones, along with Ballyman Castle and the manors of Fassaroe and Powerscourt, with their water and fishing rights. When a branch of the O'Byrnes came under sustained attack they surrendered to Henry and handed over the town of Wicklow and the Black Castle. Thomas Butler, tenth Earl of Ormonde, advised the king that the *first fruits* (the first harvest, given as a tax to the Church) of the see of Dublin should go towards the repair of the Black Castle and Arklow Castle. The O'Byrnes and O'Tooles destroyed Powerscourt House and many properties of the Crown in Cos. Wicklow and Kildare.

Another beneficiary of King Henry's policy in Ireland was Sir William Brabazon. In 1540 many religious orders were forced to surrender their lands and property to the Crown. Five years later, Brabazon, a soldier and statesman of Anglo-Norman lineage, then Lord Justice and Treasurer, was granted the lands of the Kingdom of St Thomas, together with all their properties and jurisdictions. A section of the property consisted of the lands of Kilruddery at Bray, where the monks had built a large rural retreat and burial ground. Brabazon was granted the patent of Kilruddery at the yearly rent of £8 6s 8d, together with two foot soldiers for the defence of the property, an estate near Laragh and a sizable property near Aughrim. When he died, in 1552, his son, a Privy Councillor to Queen Elizabeth I and member of Parliament for Wicklow, was created Baron Ardee.

By the end of the reign of King Henry VIII most of the religious houses within the Pale were dissolved. Outside the Pale, the Reformation generally proved unsuccessful.

FIACHA MAC AODHA Ó BROIN

From the middle of the sixteenth century the chief of the O'Byrnes, Fiacha mac Aodha Ó Broin (more popularly called Fiach MacHugh O'Byrne), son of Aodh mac Sheáin Ó Broin, was the most formidable member of the sept. Following the Anglo-Norman invasion this branch of the O'Byrnes was compelled to retire to the mountains on the western side of Ranelagh or Kilconnell, which later became known as Fiach's Country. In 1569 Fiach MacHugh assisted Sir Edmund Butler in escaping from Dublin Castle. Two years later, when he launched an attack on the Pale, his fame quickly spread. From his stronghold in Ballinacor at the head of Glenmalure he attacked English bases in the surrounding counties of Kildare, Carlow, Dublin, and Kilkenny. He kidnapped the sheriff of Kildare, Maurice Fitzjames, and released him only on payment of a ransom. The English vowed to end Fiach's reign and launched many expeditions against him.

In 1578 the authorities made another attempt to shire the territory and create a new county of Wicklow. They appointed Sir Henry Harrington as *seneschal* (steward). He was granted Co. Wicklow's largest estate, of 32,000 hectares (70,400 acres), covering extensive woodlands between Tinahely and Shillelagh. He named the land the Malton estate, and the woods supplied oak for many important buildings in England, including the roof of Westminster Abbey. When Lord Fitzwilliam inherited the property he changed the name to Coolattin.

The following year many of the Anglo-Irish lords in Munster, assisted by a small Italian and Spanish force, staged an uprising. They were opposed and defeated by a strong English force. Their families were evicted, and their lands were planted with English settlers. Spurred on by this success, the English hoped to achieve a similar one in Co.

Wicklow. In August 1580 a force of about a thousand horse and foot soldiers set out from Rathdrum under the command of the Lord Deputy, Arthur Grey, Lord Grey de Wilton, with orders to finally end the activities of the O'Byrnes in Glenmalure. A large group of Irish under Fiach MacHugh set up an ambush on each side of the glen and attacked the soldiers with muskets and pikes. The battle lasted half an hour and resulted in the loss of more than eight hundred lives. Grey led the survivors in defeat back to Dublin. The officers were buried at a place known as the Giant's Grave, and the lower ranks were buried in a mass grave nearby. Once again the authorities postponed the plan for a new county.

When Fiach MacHugh's house at Greenan was attacked and burned, he succeeded in evading capture. In 1581 he was pardoned for a second time. There were many accounts of his exploits. In March 1589 he captured the wife of the constable of Arklow Castle, Hugh Duff O'Donnell. Fiach and his ally Lord Baltinglass were responsible for the escape of many Irish prisoners from Dublin Castle.

The ESCAPE OF 'RED HUGH' O'DONNELL

In the 1580s the O'Donnells of Donegal were one of the most powerful septs in the country. The authorities feared that they and other septs would be assisted by a Spanish invasion. The Lord Deputy of Dublin, Sir John Perrott, captured Aodh Rua ('Red Hugh') O'Donnell, son of Sir Hugh O'Donnell. The intention was to hold him hostage in return for co-operation from his father. Red Hugh was imprisoned in a tower in Dublin Castle, but in 1590 he and some companions escaped. With the assistance of a supporter, he trekked on foot across the mountains to Roundwood, where he was recaptured and returned to Dublin Castle.

On Christmas Night 1591 Red Hugh, with Art O'Neill, Prince of Tyrone, and his brother Henry, made a second daring escape from Dublin Castle by cutting through their chains with a file. With the help of a servant Red Hugh followed the route of his earlier escape. Henry became separated from them as they made their way in a blizzard over the Wicklow Mountains. The trek also proved too strenuous for Art, who collapsed. Red Hugh sheltered with him as the servant brought news of their plight to Glenmalure. Fiach MacHugh O'Byrne, who had given protection to many escaped prisoners, now came to their rescue. He sent some of his men with food and clothes, but they found the two men frozen under a blanket of snow. Red Hugh suffered so badly from frostbite that he had to have several toes amputated. He recovered, but Art O'Neill died of exposure. Red Hugh stayed with Fiach until he was well enough to return to Co. Donegal. The Parliament in Dublin made him Earl of Tyrone.

The LEGACY OF FIACH MACHUGH

In 1594 Fiach's sons attacked and burned the house of the sheriff of Kildare, as a result of which Fiach was proclaimed a traitor, with a reward of £150 for his capture. The new Lord Deputy, Sir William Russell, continued his pursuit of Fiach, who succeeded in eluding capture. He attempted to recruit a new force from the rival forces of the O'Byrnes, but the majority of Críoch Bhranach would not support him. On 8 May, Russell again marched on Fiach, who this time was betrayed and captured. Immediately he was beheaded, and as a deterrent his head was impaled on the gates of Dublin Castle. Fiach was succeeded by his son Féilim, who, together with his brother Réamann, continued the war.

The same year a new Lord Lieutenant, Robert Devereux, Earl of Essex, arrived in Dublin with 16,000 foot and 1,300 horse soldiers, the largest army ever assembled in Ireland. His mission was to subdue the rebels in Munster and Leinster. He succeeded in capturing Caher Castle in Co. Tipperary and then marched north to confront Spanish ships in Lough Foyle. He ordered Sir Henry Harrington to deal with the problem in Co. Wicklow. On 28 May 1599 Harrington and a force of five hundred foot and fifty horse set out from Wicklow to rout the O'Byrnes. In a bloody battle at Deputy's Pass, between Wicklow and Rathdrum, Féilim and Réamann Ó Broin defeated Harrington's force. The Crown pardoned four hundred of Réamann's men, but he could not reach an agreement with the Butlers of Ormonde, and the conflict continued. About this time the strength of the O'Byrnes, the O'Tooles and their supporters in the district was put at three hundred foot soldiers and two hundred horsemen.

WICKLOW BECOMES A COUNTY

The Tudors made many unsuccessful attempts to 'shire' Wicklow, but the defeat of the Irish chiefs at Kinsale in 1601 was to prove a turning point. The authorities set about dispossessing the traditional landholders, particularly the O'Byrnes and the O'Tooles. The O'Byrnes' holdings had been greatly reduced, and their remaining territory came under the full control of Dublin Castle. In 1603 King James I of England granted the Powerscourt estate to a military adventurer, Sir Richard Wingfield. In 1606 Co. Wicklow was finally created the last county in Ireland. As a result, the barony of Rathdown was divided between Cos. Dublin and Wicklow. The county, comprising 494,704 statute acres (200,202 hectares) and extending 40 miles (64 kilometres) from north to south and 30 miles (42 kilometres) from east to west, was divided into eight baronies.

5 The EARLY MODERN PERIOD

ON 30 MARCH 1613 King James I granted a charter to the town of Wicklow. It declared that

> *the aforesaid town of Wicklow and all and singular castles, messuages, lofts, houses, buildings, waters, rivers, lands, tenements, hereditaments with their appurtenances being and lying within the said town of Wicklow (the castle of the said town of Wicklow with the privileges thereonto belonging only excepted) be and for ever hereafter shall be one entire and free borough of itself, by the name of the borough of Wicklow.*

The charter granted the new borough the power of returning two members to Parliament. Local government of a sort was established; a *portreeve* (ruler or mayor) was appointed to encourage freemen and merchants to establish their trades in the new corporate town. Hitherto agriculture had been the chief source of income, but now a livelihood could be achieved by those carrying on trade as drapers, tailors, tanners, dyers, butchers, mercers, and vintners. From among their ranks twelve burgesses emerged to represent the citizens and to encourage trade. Guilds, established to promote trade, became an influential force in local administration.

The first portreeve of Wicklow was Patrick Conway, who arranged an election in which John Wolferson and Patrick Barnewall were elected. However, this election was declared void by the government of the day, on the grounds that Conway himself had not been properly appointed. A new portreeve, Sir Arthur Usher, was appointed and, with royal permission, held a new election, which returned Sir William Usher (the then Constable of the Castle of Wicklow) and Sir Lawrence Esmonde as Wicklow's first representatives in Parliament.

Markets were held on Saturdays for the sale of meat, poultry, and vegetables. There was no need for a corn market, as corn was delivered whenever it was available. Races were held at low tide on a long stretch of strand on the Murrough, the narrow peninsula enclosing a creek north of the harbour. Fairs were held on 28 March, 24 May, 12 August, and 25 November.

Coinciding with the historic shiring of Wicklow was the Church of Ireland's plan to extend its organisation throughout the county. Its numbers were then low, and it had limited resources for recruiting new clergymen. The Catholic Church, on the other hand, had a large number of priests and still received patronage from the native Irish lords. In 1615 a secret synod was arranged in Kilkenny in order to stem the English effort to destroy Catholicism with the seizure and destruction of churches. One of the prime objectives of the synod was to reorganise parishes. In 1630 in north Wicklow there existed the two parishes of Kilmacanogue and Connaught. As a result the small parish of Bray, with the larger parishes of Stagonil (Powerscourt), Kilcroney, Kilruddery, Templecarrig, and the district of Kilmacanogue were formed into one parish under one priest. It became known as the parish of Kilmacanogue and Bray, with Father Dermot Byrne as the first parish priest.

To ensure a stronger foothold for the Church of Ireland, a series of restrictions was imposed on Catholic worship throughout the country. The influence of the Catholic Church was greatly diminished, while that of the Church of Ireland was strengthened. English planters received grants of land in Co. Wicklow, and by 1640 the proportion of land in the county owned by Catholics had dipped below half as a result of the policy of confiscation and plantation.

During November 1641 Luke O'Toole of Castlekevin attacked the Black Castle in Wicklow town. In retaliation, Sir Charles Coote and his soldiers set fire to a small church in which local people had sought refuge, and they were burned to death. Thereafter the area became known as Melancholy Lane. Following the Rising of 1641 many English settlers in north Wicklow were driven out of their land.

The CROMWELLIAN CAMPAIGN

In 1649, following the Civil War in England and the execution of King Charles I, the English administration once more turned its attention to Ireland. The new Lord Lieutenant, Oliver Cromwell, and a large force arrived in Dublin to implement a campaign of transforming the nature of the landed aristocracy in Ireland. Cromwell engaged in widespread slaughter as he gave Catholic Irish landlords the ultimatum of 'to Hell or to Connacht,' transferring their property to Protestant ownership. But it was only the rich Catholic landlords who were seen as the enemy, and most of the poor were left untouched. Estates throughout Co. Wicklow were to suffer during this campaign, and their landlords were banished. Cromwell's Puritans were as hard on Irish Protestants as they were on Catholics.

Another target of the campaign was the property of the Catholic Church itself, and Cromwell's soldiers attacked and destroyed many churches, chapels, and monasteries. A price was put on the head of priests. Cromwell first captured Drogheda and massacred the entire garrison of 3,500 royalists. Following the massacre he and his army marched south through Bray and stayed in Killincarrig Castle. Many of Cromwell's officers and adventurers were given allocations of land and remained in Ireland. The Cromwellian Plantation caused two-thirds of the land in the country to change hands and ended the activities of many of the defiant septs, including the O'Byrnes and the O'Tooles.

In 1653 an act was passed by the English Parliament that confiscated all land in Ireland. As a result all grants, deeds, and patents became worthless. For the English government, the military campaign in Ireland had proved costly. Debenture-holders who had financed the war demanded to be paid, and army officers who had fought in the Cromwellian campaign were also claiming overdue wages. Land in four counties–Wicklow, Donegal, Leitrim, and Longford–was earmarked to raise the arrears due.

Following the plantation and confiscation of lands and assets under King James I, most of Co. Wicklow was in the hands of people considered loyal to the Crown, and the county was no longer seen as a threat. Though lands were transferred under royal authority, there was great confusion about the actual ownership of some land, with much sub-division and sub-letting. Feuds frequently arose over land rights, as the country had never been accurately mapped. In 1654 an English army physician, William Petty, was offered the task of mapping the entire country. He employed soldiers to do the measuring of land, and the maps became known as the Down Survey. The maps for Co. Wicklow are most interesting and clearly show mountain ranges, rivers, castles, and big houses.

The Act of Settlement (1661) confirmed Cromwell's new settlers in their holdings, while at the same time any of the dispossessed who could prove they were innocent of any complicity in the Rising of 1641 were to be reinstated. Cromwellian soldiers were permitted to hold their land; if they were displaced they would receive alternative lands of equal size. Catholic landowners succeeded in reclaiming only part of their original holdings. In 1666 Lord Meath and Lord Tyrconnell agreed on the partitioning of Bray. This settlement led to better understanding and fewer hostilities and encouraged people to rent plots and to extend the town.

One of the earliest catamarans was built in Arklow in 1663. Sir William Petty, Marquis of Lansdowne, had seen the twin-hulled 'kattamaran' in the Indian Ocean and placed an order with an Arklow boatbuilder. This strange craft made its first voyage across the Irish Sea in July 1664. There is a model in the Science Museum in London.

The PENAL LAWS

In 1685, when King Charles II died, his brother, the Catholic James II, replaced him. The Catholics of Ireland felt they would be better treated under his regime; but they were mistaken. In 1695 the activities of Catholics were restricted under a series of penal laws imposed by the Parliament. These were designed to eradicate the Catholic religion in Ireland and to secure the privileged position of the Church of Ireland, the established church. They imposed restrictions on education, the bearing of arms, the purchase of land, holding commissions in the army or navy, entering the legal profession, holding any government office, and taking a seat in Parliament.

Under Queen Anne a law was passed whereby all Catholic clergy had to be registered. This forced many priests underground, while others were allowed to operate on condition that they urge their congregations to support the authorities. It was intended that registered priests could be kept under a watchful eye, while the absence of bishops would prevent ordinations. To escape the restrictions many young men travelled to the Continent to attend seminaries there; Father Richard Fitzsimons, for example, was ordained in Flanders in 1682 to minister to the parish of Kilmacanogue.

There was a policy in Dublin Castle of rewarding informers who reported unregistered priests, and small group of extremists forced the authorities to apply the penal laws in all its severity. There were only thirteen registered priests in Co. Wicklow. The most notorious 'priest-hunter' in the county was Edward Tyrrell, who was responsible for the naming and arrest of many underground priests. Some families braved these restrictions and gave shelter to outlawed priests; they were prepared to risk loss of property and even imprisonment to allow priests to celebrate Mass secretly in their homes. Most notable among these were the Eustaces of Oldcourt and the Walshes of Old Connaught, near Enniskerry. Many Protestants also saw the injustice of these laws. One landlord, the Earl of Meath, gave the parish priest of Bray refuge, and workers on the estate attended Mass in an outhouse; but no priest ministered publicly in Bray for many years.

In June 1714 an army patrol from Wicklow under the command of the High Sheriff halted the St Kevin's *pattern* (the celebration of a saint's feast day on 3 June) at Glendalough, dispersing the pilgrims, confiscating crosses, and pulling down tents. There were many reports throughout the county of raids by soldiers on gatherings at Mass houses and Mass rocks. In 1716 there is a record of Father Owen McFee, at the age of seventy-two, being imprisoned in Wicklow Gaol and sentenced to transportation to an English colony for celebrating Mass contrary to the law.

But the authorities found it difficult to enforce many of the penal laws, and there was a gradual relaxation. By the middle of the eighteenth century permission was being given for the erection of a number of small chapels in Co. Wicklow, though these primitive buildings had to be built off the main streets and out of sight. Some of the more intransigent landlords placed further restrictions, insisting that churches be built at least a mile outside towns under their control. Examples of such churches are those of Curtlestown (1824), St Peter's, Little Bray (1837), Wicklow (1844), and Enniskerry (1860).

From 1774 to 1793 a series of Relief Acts began to repeal the penal laws; but it was not until 1829, with the passing of the Catholic Relief Act, promoted by Daniel O'Connell, that all restrictions on Catholics were removed. This enabled Catholics to sit in Parliament, belong to any corporation, and hold higher state offices.

WICKLOW GAOL

By the beginning of the eighteenth century each county was obliged by law to have a gaol in its main town. In 1702 work began at Kilmantan Hill on Wicklow Gaol, which was to become one of the most menacing places in Co. Wicklow during this period. The commonest form of hard labour in the gaol was the treadmill, used for pumping water or grinding wheat. The cells were not heated, and the cold in winter was the worst form of punishment. The local authority paid gaolers a small wage, from which they were to provide accommodation and food. Some of these gaolers were open to bribery, and prisoners had to pay them to receive preferential treatment. A committee appointed to examine conditions in the gaol reported that the place had not seen a whitewash brush for years. 'It was deadly, pitch dark and utterly unfit for human habitation.' The gaol housed all kinds of people in the eighteenth century, from pickpockets to murderers. Large crowds attended the hangings in Wicklow, which were always held in public, in an attempt to deter those who might have a mind to break the law. The gallows was erected at Friars Hill.

The worst feature of Wicklow Gaol was the severity of the sentences handed down by the magistrates. Paupers appearing before the court received lengthy terms for stealing clothes or food. A report in 1820 noted that there were nine public hangings on one day. The nine local men had fallen on hard times and had stolen clothes from neighbouring clotheslines. They were sentenced to death, but no date could be set for the hanging, as the hangman travelled like a journeyman from gaol to gaol enquiring, 'How many have you got today?' One of the gaol's most distinguished prisoners was Erskine Childers senior, who was imprisoned there in 1922.

6 From GRATTAN To PARNELL

HENRY GRATTAN, born in Dublin in 1746, became a distinguished lawyer. In 1775 he entered the Irish Parliament and quickly became a vocal advocate of Irish independence. When the Parliament gained a degree of independence he demanded that Ireland should be granted its rightful status as an independent country.

Long before Grattan came to live in Enniskerry he had loved that part of Co. Wicklow and had made frequent visits there. In 1779 he attended a meeting at the seashore in Bray at which he completed an address to Parliament. By his brilliant oratory Grattan became the leader of the movement to repeal Poynings' Law (which made the actions of the Irish Parliament subject to the approval of the Privy Council in London). Grattan was successful, and the law was almost completely repealed, the only part of it remaining being the Crown's right to veto a bill.

During this period a series of Catholic Relief Acts (1774–93) were enacted, which repealed the penal laws. Under these acts Catholics were permitted to buy and own land and to practise law, and the bar on Catholics receiving university degrees was removed.

For eighteen years, from 16 April 1782 to 2 August 1800, 'Grattan's Parliament' enjoyed virtual independence. The name is ironic, as

Grattan was always a member of the opposition. He represented Dublin in the British House of Commons from 1806 until his death. In 1784 the British government voted £100,000 to Grattan for his services to the Crown. Reluctantly, Grattan accepted half that amount, with which he bought and converted an old coaching inn at Tinnahinch, outside Enniskerry, into a mansion.

During the 1798 Rising the insurgents and the authorities were equally anxious that Grattan's name be among those of the insurgents. In Grattan's absence some Yeomen called to Tinnahinch and stated that they had proof of his treason. Lord Powerscourt ordered the soldiers to disperse and not to molest Grattan's wife, and they confined themselves to burning the orchard. Following the Battle of Arklow, soldiers stopped at the house, where some of the party wanted to blow it up, but the majority were against it.

After the Act of Union, Grattan retired to Tinnahinch and devoted himself to study and the education of his children.

The 1798 RISING

With growing unrest throughout the county, the County Wicklow Regiment of Militia was established in 1793. Every town and village had an infantry company, while the Cavalry Corps were based in Arklow, Baltinglass, Bray, Dunlavin, Powerscourt, Rathdrum, Shillelagh, Newtown Mount Kennedy (today known as Newtownmountkennedy), and Upper and Lower Talbotstown.

In 1794 the Society of United Irishmen was established in the hope of gaining economic and political independence for Ireland. Though Theobald Wolfe Tone and most other founder-members were Protestants, they sought a non-sectarian independent republic, with equal rights for Catholics. When the government banned its activities it was transformed into a secret society, with a large influx of Catholic members.

The United Irishmen, who were influenced by the French Revolution, adopted short hair in the French style and were soon nicknamed 'Croppies'. Unrest spread through the country, and the leaders of the United Irishmen requested French aid to support an uprising. In December 1796 forty warships carrying fifteen thousand men sailed from France; but through a series of misfortunes, including storms and shipwrecks, the venture failed. Meanwhile there followed more repressive action by the authorities.

In September 1797 additional militia forces were sent to Co. Wicklow to combat rumblings of agitation in the area. In October 1797 a loyalist officer of the Antrim Militia, Major Joseph Hardy, was appointed district commander of west Wicklow and areas of Cos. Wexford and Carlow. His main objective was to contain the activities of the United Irishmen at all costs. Spies infiltrated the movement and sent reports to Dublin Castle. Acting on this information, Hardy arrested suspected United Irishmen and seized large quantities of pikes and some muskets in west Wicklow. During this period, pikes (long staves with a spearhead and a hook on top) were the main weapons of the insurgents. As similar pikes were in daily use as farm implements, they at first drew no suspicion. They could be manufactured cheaply by local blacksmiths and were light to carry and easily transportable by men who had no access to horses. In addition they could be concealed in fields or rivers, or in the thatched roof of a cabin. The pike proved itself a serviceable weapon in hand-to-hand combat, when a large force of men could charge the enemy at point-blank range. Many blacksmiths were arrested under suspicion of being rebel sympathisers.

Hardy had at his disposal 1,000 regular soldiers and 1,250 Yeomen (a volunteer cavalry made up of large farmers); he also had 2,200 untrained and poorly disciplined 'supplementary' Yeomen. The most severe repressive measures were undertaken against the civilian population by the Ancient Britons, a Welsh cavalry regiment under the command of Sir Watkin William Wynne, whose name became a byword for repression and butchery.

In November the barony of Talbotstown was placed under martial law, and the ill-treatment of the community that followed provoked fear and anger. The United Irishmen were still hoping for help from France before starting a rising, but Hardy's campaign of torture and intimidation was pushing them to breaking point. Hardy requested Captain John Edwards, commander of the Rathdown Cavalry, based in Bray, to send reinforcements to south Wicklow. Edwards refused to assist in this repressive campaign and declined to enforce this policy in north Wicklow.

By January 1798 the recruiting and training of the United Irishmen in Co. Wicklow was proceeding apace. Tom King, commander of Yeomanry in Rathdrum, devised a test of loyalty and allegiance to flush out any supporters of the United Irishmen among their ranks. There were so many United men in the ranks of the Cronebane Yeomanry, near Avoca, in Hardy's opinion that he disbanded it.

On 11 April 1798, during the annual fair in Newtownmountkennedy, a force of Redcoats launched a random attack, slashing at any woman wearing green. Eight men suspected of being rebels were arrested and were hanged without trial. This atrocity was to incense the community, and many more joined the ranks of the United Irishmen. The following month United Irishmen of the eight baronies of Co. Wicklow were instructed by the leadership to rise and launch attacks against the Crown forces in Cos. Kildare, Dublin, and Carlow. Some of the Wicklow insurgents joined with the United Irishmen of north Wexford. Hardy intensified his campaign against the insurgents, imposing martial law, burning property, and torturing suspects. The authorities hoped that such measures as public floggings would break the resilience of the insurgents. Hardy's campaign ensured that only a small proportion of Co. Wicklow's fourteen thousand United Irishmen joined the rising. Most were armed only with pikes and muskets, against the cannons and artillery of the Crown forces. Co. Wicklow magistrates issued an appeal for the surrender of arms, failing which more severe measures would be applied against the population.

The United Irishmen became more determined and held a secret council to bring forward the date of the national uprising. On 23 May the Wicklow insurgents began operations by choosing vulnerable targets and attempting to cut communications with Dublin. They launched surprise attacks on the small garrisons at Ballymore Eustace and Stratford, inflicting heavy losses on the Ancient Britons and the Yeomen. However, when they approached Baltinglass the Crown forces had been reinforced and were waiting for them. The insurgents found themselves trapped between Crown forces from the town and another force from Stratford. More than two hundred insurgents were killed in this badly planned attack. When news of the attack reached Ballymore Eustace, Crown forces feared an attack on the Dunlavin garrison. A force of Ancient Britons and local Yeomanry took up strategic positions and defended the village. Again the insurgents were defeated, with a loss of three hundred men. Captain Richardson took the decision to put to death thirty-five insurgents held in Dunlavin Jail as a reprisal; the men were tied together and shot on Dunlavin Green. Only one man survived the massacre, by pretending to be dead when he was wounded.

On 29 May a large force of insurgents gathered to attack Newtownmountkennedy. Learning from the failure of some earlier attacks, the insurgents of Newcastle and Ballinacor North launched a pincer attack on the town with a force of about a thousand men. The town was strongly defended by a large force of Ancient Britons, with the Antrim Militia and the local Yeomanry under the command of Captain Burgany in support. The insurgents succeeded in breaking the outer defence and reached the town centre, but in a counter-attack they were forced to retreat. Burgany was killed in the encounter. Inmates of the local guardhouse were put to death in reprisal.

The next day, in a follow-up operation led by Hardy in the Devil's Glen and Dunran Woods, many insurgents were massacred; others lying wounded died when the cavalry set fire to the forest. This defeat greatly depleted the insurgent force in north Wicklow. Following the funeral of Captain Burgany and his soldiers in Newtownmountkennedy, the Ancient Britons and local Yeomen went on a rampage, killing people at will and setting fire to buildings. Sir James Duff led a force of the Sixth Dragoons and the Dublin City Militia against the insurgents' camp at Blackmore Hill, but they withdrew to the safety of the Wicklow Mountains.

In Carnew, sixty-one men who had been accused of being rebels but had been acquitted were rearrested and imprisoned in Carnew Castle. On 1 June, Lieutenant Patten of the Antrim Militia ordered that forty-one of the prisoners be brought from the guardhouse to the ball alley, where they were shot. A week later the insurgents sought retaliation when they attacked and burned the town. News of the two massacres spread throughout the countryside, fuelling the worst fears of local people that there would be a campaign of slaughter.

On 9 June two columns of insurgents, armed largely with pikes, led by Father Michael Murphy of Ballycanew, Billy Byrne of Ballymanus, and Anthony Perry of Inch staged an attack from the south on Crown forces in Arklow. The town was garrisoned by 1,400 English, Scottish and Irish soldiers under the command of General Needham and Lieutenant-General Lake. In the day-long battle the insurgents charged the Crown lines, suffering heavy losses. Despite repeated attacks and destroying the cannons, the insurgents, armed only with pikes and muskets, failed to take the town, and following the death of Father Murphy and seven hundred men, they retreated. The Redcoats cut out Father Murphy's heart and burned it. The insurgent leader Joseph Holt and his force were more successful in the Glendalough and Roundwood area, where they burned more than twenty loyalists' houses. They carried out hit-and-run attacks on vulnerable targets and kept the Crown forces occupied in pursuit.

The insurgents regrouped at Gorey Hill, from where, on 17 June, they launched an attack on Tinahely. The garrison, under Generals Dundas and Loftus, realised they were outnumbered and abandoned the town. The insurgents burned the town in retaliation for the behaviour of the Yeomen.

Over the next three months the insurgents were active in a number of south Wicklow towns. Forces under the command of Joseph Holt ambushed a force of Redcoats and inflicted numerous casualties but failed to take the garrison at Carnew. In early July they killed nineteen Yeomen in a battle on Ballyrahan Hill, near Tinahely. In one of the final strikes by the insurgents in Co. Wicklow they captured and burned buildings in Aughrim.

On 15 October 1798 another Battle of Glenmalure began when General Eustace and eighty Redcoats were on patrol in the glen. Insurgents under the command of Michael Dwyer, who had been observing them, chose the moment when the patrol was most vulnerable to attack. They suddenly surfaced above them and opened fire. The soldiers retreated, but the insurgents pursued them, keeping up constant fire for three miles. Eustace was forced to return to barracks in defeat and later claimed in his report that he was outnumbered. He returned the following day with five hundred men, but Dwyer had withdrawn into the safety of the mountains, where he had established his headquarters.

Historians have never been able to fully explain why the fighting in 1798 was particularly ferocious in Co. Wicklow. At its height there were fourteen thousand United Irishmen in the county, more than any other county in Leinster. At that time Co. Wicklow had the largest rural Protestant population outside Ulster. These were educated people, familiar with European culture and exposed to the liberal thinking of the Enlightenment and later the French Revolution. Dublin Castle did not fully trust the Co. Wicklow magistrates, who they feared might be too tolerant in dealing with dissent in the county.

This period ended with the murder of a parish priest, Archdeacon Andrew O'Toole. In the late 1700s Father O'Toole came to Co. Wicklow, having lived abroad for many years. He struck up a friendship with Lord Fitzwilliam, one of the largest landlords in Co. Wicklow. When O'Toole approached him about getting an abbey for a parochial residence, Fitzwilliam agreed, but there were objections from extremists, and the solicitor held up the transfer of deeds. On 12 June 1799 the parochial residence was burned to the ground, and Father O'Toole had to flee. On 27 August he was returning to his home in Croneroe (later the Belair Hotel) when he was set upon by three men and strangled. An old woman gathering sticks witnessed the murder, but she disappeared and was never seen again. The culprits were never caught.

The rising continued in Co. Wicklow for years after it was suppressed elsewhere in the country. The authorities in Dublin declared that Wicklow was still 'the most disturbed county in Ireland.' It was not until 1803 that the English finally established control of the area. By then approximately 106 men had been transported from Co. Wicklow to the penal colonies of New South Wales. This was more than from any other county: six hundred was the estimated number of transportations for the entire country.

MICHAEL DWYER

Michael Dwyer was born in the townland of Camara in the Glen of Imail in 1772, the eldest of seven children of a small farmer. He attended a local hedge school, and in 1797 he joined the United Irishmen and became active in the movement. Before the rising he had gone on the run and quickly displayed his leadership while fighting in the Battles of Arklow and Vinegar Hill and leading the insurgents in the Battle of Hacketstown. When the rising was put down, Dwyer retreated with a loyal group of supporters into the Wicklow Mountains, where he was appointed 'Governor of Glenmalure' and was also known as 'Master of the Mountains'.

Dwyer evaded capture for five years and ran a successful guerrilla campaign against the Redcoats, maintaining the constant hope that there would be a French invasion. He had many narrow escapes. On 15 February 1799 he and his companions were resting in a cottage at

Derrynamuck when a strong force of Redcoats surrounded it. Samuel McAllister drew the fire of the soldiers, allowing the others to escape. The courageous McAllister and three others were killed and eight were captured. The prisoners were put to death, except for one, who turned informer. Dwyer, always a good tactician, made his way barefoot across the snow.

On another occasion, Dwyer came around a bend on horseback with two companions near Castleruddery. About a hundred yards ahead of them they saw a line of Redcoats. Instantly Dwyer shouted, 'Come on, lads, up and at them,' giving the impression that there was an army behind him. The soldiers turned and retreated. On another occasion Dwyer held up a force of Redcoats with a small group and managed to take their arms.

When Dwyer first went on the run there was a bounty of £300 on his head, but this gradually increased to £500. He was a hero among the local people, who supported him by relaying messages for him and leaving food at designated places, such as at Brusher's Gate, near Lough Dan.

Dwyer was aware that the government was constructing a Military Road through the mountains that would give its forces quicker ingress into the hills, further weakening his position. News reached him in 1803 of the disheartening failure of Robert Emmet's rising in Dublin. Dwyer's niece Anne Devlin was in the employ of Emmet and had carried messages back and forth between them. Dwyer, a realist, quick to realise the futility of his situation and anxious to avoid further unnecessary bloodshed, surrendered to William Hume, the member of Parliament for Co. Wicklow. Hume agreed that Dwyer and his group would be sent to North America, but the government failed to honour the agreement, and Dwyer and his men were sent to a penal colony in New South Wales, though as free settlers. In July 1805 Dwyer, his wife and the other insurgents, including Hugh 'Vesty' Byrne, sailed in the prison ship *Tillicherry* from Cóbh, Co. Cork. Seven years later Dwyer was appointed constable for an area known as Liverpool, near Sydney, and he also became a farmer. He died on 23 August 1825 and was buried in Sydney.

BILLY BYRNE

In the Square in Wicklow there is a memorial to a local hero, Billy Byrne, who had led a group of insurgents at the Battle of Vinegar Hill on 21 June 1798. He had fought earlier that month alongside his older brother, Garrett, in the Battle of Arklow.

Billy Byrne was born in 1775, the youngest son of Garrett Byrne of Ballymanus. The Byrnes was one of the last Catholic families still in possession of their land in Co. Wicklow. Billy was a reluctant hero, who took part in the fight only after much provocation, having been incensed at the treatment meted out to people in the district. He was arrested and court-martialled on the charge of being a rebel leader and spent six months in Wicklow Gaol under sentence of death. It was expected that this sentence would be commuted to transportation, but the Byrnes had influential enemies. Paid informers gave evidence against him and he was hanged on Gallows Hill on 21 September 1799. The Byrnes were dispossessed of their land and property as a result of their son's participation in the rising.

JOSEPH HOLT

Joseph Holt was an important leader in the 1798 Rising. He joined the insurgents after the destruction of his house and farm by the Fermanagh Militia on 10 May. His greatest victory was defeating a force of Ancient Britons in an ambush at the Battle of Ballyellis. A large reward was offered for his capture, but he held out in the mountains, leading attacks on patrols and convoys while waiting for the promised French aid. When this did not materialise, his wife negotiated terms of surrender for him. Holt was transported to New South Wales as a free man, with permission to bring his wife and family. He continued to take part in Irish schemes in Australia.

The MILITARY ROAD

The British government realised that its forces would need a good road through the Wicklow Mountains if they were to defeat the insurgents on their own territory. The boggy terrain made it impossible to move heavy weapons and equipment to where they were needed. The elusive tactics of Michael Dwyer and his insurgents were embarrassing and frustrating for local commanders and Yeomen; the construction of a road, though expensive, was necessary if they were ever to gain control of the mountains. In August 1800 work began on the 35-mile (56-kilometre) road through the heart of the Wicklow Mountains from Rathfarnham, Co. Dublin, to Aughavanagh. Two hundred soldiers of the Highland Regiment were put to work, at a shilling per day; their supervising officers where paid five shillings a day; local labourers who boosted their numbers were paid a penny a day. At first good progress was made, but the bitter winter slowed the work.

In 1803 the first phase of the road was completed, linking Glencree through the Sally Gap to Roundwood and Glendalough. The engineers were anxious not to incur any unnecessary expense, so the road followed the contour of the hills wherever possible, eliminating the need for large bridges. The complete road network was not finished until 1809.

Many impressive barracks and blockhouses were constructed along the route of the Military Road, approximately one day's march apart. On 3 March 1803 the *Freeman's Journal* reported: 'At the Glen of Imaal there is to be a barracks for a field officer and 200 men; at Glencree a captain and 100; at Laragh a captain and 100; at Glenmalure the same and at Aughavanagh the same.' Of these five buildings only two are still used today: that at Aughavanagh is a youth hostel, and that at Glencree is used by the Glencree Centre for Reconciliation. Stories abound that revolutionaries in a campaign against the Royal Irish Constabulary burned the ruined Drumgoff Barracks at Glenmalure in 1920, but in fact the building had been crumbling since 1820, when the Redcoats departed.

The largest of the barracks on the Military Road, Glencree Barracks, has a commanding view of Glencree Valley stretching to the sea, and the strong garrison was in contact with the vital southernmost martello tower at Bray. The buildings have undergone many incarnations. In 1858 they were acquired by the Oblate Fathers and opened as the first reformatory in Ireland for young offenders. During the Second World War the buildings were a centre for refugee children fleeing the conflict in Europe under the umbrella of the Red Cross. In more recent times they have been renovated and are the home of the Glencree Centre for Reconciliation. In the intervening periods the buildings have been used as a location for historical films.

MARTELLO TOWERS

At the end of the eighteenth century there was widespread speculation that the French would launch an attack on Ireland to support the rising of the United Irishmen. As a precaution, the authorities decided to build a series of watchtowers stretching from Bray to Balbriggan in north Co. Dublin. These came to be called martello towers, after the original tower at Cap Mortella in Corsica, which had withstood an English assault in 1794. The military then used a system of flags and lights to transmit warnings and instructions, so each tower was built within signalling range of the next, thus establishing a reliable line of communication along the east coast. The towers were occupied by a small garrison and equipped with an 18-pounder gun. That three of these defences were built at Bray in 1804 showed its strategic importance as the southern defence of Dublin. The martello towers were within a day's infantry march of the new army barracks at Glencree and the start of the Military Road through the mountains.

Following the Battle of Waterloo in 1815 the threat of invasion abated, and the garrisons were considered superfluous. There is no account of any of the towers being called into action. Of the three towers in Bray only one remains today, overlooking the harbour.

The POOR LAW AND WORKHOUSES

The Poor Relief (Ireland) Act (1838) was introduced to help ease the increasing level of poverty throughout Ireland. Under this act, which was administered from London until 1847, Ireland was divided into 130 Poor Law 'unions' or groups of parishes, each centred on a market town. Each union had to provide for its own poor by means of a local 'poor rate' levied on all property within the union. Irish landlords financed this in large part. Each union built a workhouse, usually constructed according to a standard plan designed by the English architect George Wilkinson. Ratepayers elected a board of guardians, consisting of merchants, businessmen, and farmers, who were responsible for building and administering the workhouses. Each union was rated by the number of poor it sent to the workhouse; half was to be paid by the tenants and the remainder by the landlords. Priority was given to the old, the ill, and those in dire need.

The most cruel feature of the workhouses was the requirement that families, though they had to enter the workhouse as a unit (single people were not eligible for relief), were divided on admission, and no further contact between them was permitted. There was strict segregation, with separate wards for men and boys, for women and girls, and for children over two years old; only children under two could remain with their mother. There were also separate 'lunatic' and 'idiot' wards for men and women. Each workhouse had an infirmary and infirmary yard. All the inmates, who were dressed in uniforms, were required to work in the kitchen, washroom, and infirmary or to do other manual chores; the men and boys were usually employed breaking stones. Food was rationed and monotonous, consisting mainly of potatoes, porridge, and milk. Extra accommodation often had to be provided by erecting sheds at the rear of the building. A paupers' graveyard adjoined each workhouse.

Co. Wicklow was allocated five workhouses. The Rathdown Workhouse, at Loughlinstown, Co. Dublin (now St Columcille's Hospital), catered for ten electoral districts in south Co. Dublin and north Co. Wicklow, including Bray, Delgany, and Powerscourt. The Rathdrum Workhouse catered for Arklow, Newcastle, Wicklow, Rathdrum, Roundwood, and Aughrim. The workhouse at Baltinglass was responsible for Dunlavin, Donard, Hollywood, Kiltegan, and Baltinglass, while the Shillelagh workhouse catered for Carnew, Shillelagh, Coolattin, Tinahely, and parts of east Co. Carlow. The Naas Union incorporated Blessington and Baltiboys.

In Rathdrum, where the standard of living was particularly bad, the workhouse was soon overcrowded. Hundreds of destitute people besieged the building every week looking for help, but many were turned away. The Rathdrum Orphanage had a particularly high mortality rate.

FAMINE

It was fortunate that the Poor Law scheme was in existence throughout the country before the potato blight afflicted the crop of 1845. Hitherto this scheme had aided the poor, but the Great Famine was to have a serious impact throughout a wider section of society. An infrastructure existed that coped with the first impact of crop failure. Food scarcity was not unknown in Ireland, but the Great Famine of 1845–49 was to become one of the worst human catastrophes in Irish history.

The first signs of potato blight appeared in September 1845. It was hoped that it was only a partial famine, and at first there was no crisis, as there were reserves of other food. But the worst fears of the poor were realised as gradually the potato crop failed all over Ireland. This was a calamity, as the potato was the staple food of a third of the population.

Co. Wicklow was fortunate to escape the worst of the food scarcity until the following year. In October the first official reports of the potato blight in the county came from a magistrate in Baltinglass. Arklow was doubly hit, as the herring stock failed at the same time, making a replacement source of food impossible. Despite the plight of the hungry, there were no hand-outs. Food had to be earned, so the Board of Works instigated relief works, such as repairing roads and clearing ditches, to relieve the impact of the deplorable conditions of the poor. One scheme was the building of the coast road south from Wicklow. In Arklow up to 650 men were employed in a variety of relief schemes. People in the west of the county fared worst, and there were reports of the families of labourers and small farmers dying of starvation. Most extended families lived in a one-roomed mud cabin.

Meat was expensive and beyond the reach of even those with steady employment. Potatoes were the main source of protein and carbohydrates. Food rationing was introduced, and starving people besieged the workhouses, which were soon full and unable to cope. Food had to be distributed at the gate to those who could not be admitted; other families were forced into begging and poaching on the rivers to keep from starving. In some areas of Co. Wicklow, rivers were totally cleared of trout and eels.

The main problem was not just the absence of the potato but the rising cost of food, which labourers and paupers were unable to afford. The price of corn for baking bread rose sharply, putting it beyond the budget of the poor. The effect of the local relief schemes, soup kitchens, government schemes, and distribution of free food by some landlords eased the worst of the crisis in some areas. In the summer of 1846 the Arklow and Wicklow hospitals became overcrowded. A proposal by a priest in Dunlavin for the purchase of Indian corn to feed the poor was acted on, and Sir John Peel arranged for it to be imported and distributed to the poor. Stirabout or porridge made with Indian corn became known as 'Peel's brimstone'.

In Arklow that winter it was estimated that there was only enough food in the town to last four days. To survive through the winter months, fishermen were forced to pawn their tackle. Among the deaths were those of many of the carters from the Avoca and Arklow areas who brought ore from the mines to the docks in Arklow. The situation became acute, and stocks began piling up at the mines because of the lack of labour to transport the raw material. By March 1847 the number of people employed in Co. Wicklow on famine relief schemes, such as construction and repair work on roads, piers, bridges, and buildings, amounted to 6,678. With fears that farm labourers would refuse to accept normal spring and summer agricultural work for lower rates, the public works began to be phased out, and government-assisted soup kitchens were relied on to meet the needs of many of the destitute. Some Protestant groups that organised soup kitchens openly proselytised; those who changed their religion in exchange for soup or other material aid became known as 'soupers'.

Throughout the worst of the famine the needy of Bray were supplied with food and clothing by the local gentry and aristocracy. Small-scale soup kitchens were set up by some of the resident Anglo-Irish gentry before they became official policy in the spring of 1847. Lady Plunkett set up soup kitchens at Old Connaught, while her husband increased his labourers' wages to meet rising prices, from 10 shillings to 12 shillings for a sixty-hour week. In Bray, Lady Meath and Mrs Putland distributed food and clothing to the poorest families. Crowds of beggars constantly waylaid Mrs Putland at the gate when her carriage-and-four passed in and out. The parish priest, Father Roche, stated that 270 heads of families and 400 able-bodied people were urgently needed to build a road for Mr Putland, a local landlord. Putland offered employment to the destitute labourers as a famine relief scheme, the result being the Putland Road, linking the Boghall Road to the sea front. In Baltiboys, Elizabeth Smith and her husband fed twenty-two paupers each day in their courtyard. There were fewer resident landlords and middle-class people in the west of the county than on the east coast, so that more charity was available in Bray, Wicklow, and Arklow.

There was growing despair among the rural poor as parents witnessed their children starving, and they sought an escape from the scourge of famine. The poor were driven to extremes, and the crime rate rose sharply. Starving men stole from the big houses and attacked rent and rate collectors. Extra soldiers were despatched to contend with this growing unrest. To worsen their plight, some landlords began to evict pauper tenants who fell behind with their rent. Some people resettled on a common called the Black Bawns, where the families built new cabins.

The only escape for many was emigration. Fear forced many people to flee to Liverpool, London, and further afield, to Canada and the United States. The guardians of the more solvent Poor Law unions realised the advantage of the younger and healthier families emigrating, and payments were made to such families to cover their passage. The Poor Law particularly financed young women, who could find employment in service in Australia and America. But many of Co. Wicklow's poor moved no further than the slums of Dublin.

In 1847, when the Coolattin estate asked for volunteers to emigrate, more than six thousand people applied, and Lord Fitzwilliam assisted them financially in travelling to Canada. The Quakers and other religious institutions also gave financial assistance, and a priest from the Tinahely area organised a large number of people in emigrating to America. The emigration schemes undertaken by landlords became known as 'shovelling out,' as the tenants' cabins were demolished as soon as they were vacated.

There were 2,776 recorded deaths in Co. Wicklow in 1847. In 1841 the population of the county was a record 126,143 people, most of whom were dependent on agriculture. Within a decade the figure had dropped to 98,979; by 1861 it had dropped another 30 per cent, and by 1871 it had fallen dramatically to 78,697. Famine fever took its toll, as those weakened by hunger fell prey to several illnesses, including typhus (known as the black fever), cholera, scurvy, and dysentery. In 1849 in an outbreak of cholera in Bray, sixty-eight people died. In 1851 the workhouse guardians had to provide each district with at least one dispensary doctor, who gave treatment to the poor. Between 6 June 1841 and 30 March 1851, 3,649 people had contracted infectious diseases in the county. Deaths in Co. Wicklow in the decade 1841–51 amounted to 16,930.

CHARLES STEWART PARNELL

An Anglo-Irish family living a comfortable life on an estate at Rathdrum, Co. Wicklow, seems an unlikely breeding-ground for Irish patriotism. The Parnell family of Avondale was the exception, producing not one but three prominent figures in the cause of land reform: Charles Stewart Parnell, known as the 'uncrowned king of Ireland', and his sisters Fanny and Anna Parnell, founder-members of the Ladies' Land League. The family had lived in Avondale House since 1795, when Sir John Parnell inherited the estate from his cousin, Samuel Hayes. The estates in turn passed to Sir William Parnell-Hayes and his successor, John Henry Parnell.

Charles Stewart Parnell was born on 27 June 1846, one of eleven children of John Henry Parnell and Delia Tudor Stewart, an American heiress. Though having a privileged childhood, the young Charles would have been aware of the anti-British views of his outspoken mother. During his education at the University of Cambridge he often returned to Avondale, where he had an active social life, with garden parties and balls. He was also a keen sportsman and was particularly fond of hunting and regularly rode with the Wicklow Harriers. Following his graduation he travelled widely in Europe

In 1859 his father died and he inherited the Avondale estate. It seemed he would be just another landlord, shooting and riding to hounds; and he joined the local militia, the Wicklow Rifles. Then, in 1874, he approached Isaac Butt, chairman of the Irish Party in the British House of Commons, with a view to entering politics.

PARNELL AND *the* LAND LEAGUE

Parnell unsuccessfully contested a Dublin seat; undeterred, he stood again a year later and won a seat in Co. Meath. Despite much petitioning the British government was not prepared to discuss home rule for Ireland. Parnell, together with some other Irish members, operated an obstructionist policy in the House of Commons in an effort to further the Irish cause. Though not a great orator, Parnell would speak for hours on every bill, delaying the business of Parliament. His disagreement with the conciliatory approach of Isaac Butt brought the two men into conflict, resulting in Parnell succeeding Butt as chairman of the Irish Party.

In 1879 Michael Davitt founded the Irish National Land League in a reaction to the worsening conditions experienced by tenant farmers during the agricultural depression. With Parnell as its first president, the league's main objectives were to organise resistance to high rents and evictions and to allow tenant farmers to have ownership of their holdings. From its foundation the league enjoyed strong financial support among the Fenians in America. In 1880 Parnell toured the United States with John Dillon and Michael Davitt, and addressed the House of Representatives.

Following the general election of April 1880, Parnell returned as leader of a militant Irish Party in London. With increased bitterness in the Land War and the success of the Land League's activities, the Prime Minister, William Gladstone, was forced to introduce a second Land Bill for Ireland. But many Irish members, including Parnell, were still not satisfied and opposed the bill.

Parnell was arrested twice for his involvement with the Land League. On the first occasion he was discharged, but in 1881 he was imprisoned with three hundred other suspects in Kilmainham Jail, Dublin, under the Protection Act (1881)—commonly called the 'Coercion Act'. The Land League was suppressed, and the political situation deteriorated, with rent withdrawals, landlords being boycotted, and an increase in violence and evictions. Finally, in April 1882, Gladstone made an agreement with Parnell, which became known as the 'Kilmainham Treaty'. The British government agreed to amend the Land Act to allow leaseholders into court to help tenants to pay off arrears, to stop coercion, and to release those arrested on suspicion of land agitation. The 'Three Fs' (fair rents, fixity of tenure, and free sale) were incorporated in the law. A land purchase scheme was established, providing a 75 per cent loan to tenants wishing to buy their holdings. Parnell, in return, agreed to help calm the unrest and to co-operate with reform measures.

A more draconian Coercion Bill brought demands from Irish agitators to revive the Land League. Parnell resisted, and in October 1882 he founded the Irish National League, a political organisation that placed home rule ahead of land reform. The formation of the National League marked the emergence of Parnell as the undisputed leader of nationalist Ireland. Eventually Gladstone came to the decision that home rule was necessary for peace in Ireland, and in 1886 the first Home Rule Bill, proposing the setting up of a parliament in Dublin, was introduced.

In his personal life Parnell also faced problems. Revelations in the divorce court in November 1890 of his love affair with Katharine O'Shea, a married woman, drew strong opposition from the Irish hierarchy and from Parnell's political colleagues, and he was ousted from the leadership of the Irish Party. On 25 June 1891 he married Katharine O'Shea, who had been divorced by her husband, and they took up residence in Brighton. But there was a rapid decline in Parnell's health, and he died in Brighton on 6 October 1891, aged forty-five.

The GENTRY AND LOCAL DEMOCRACY

By the nineteenth century, Co. Wicklow was a place of rebellion, and many landlords had recruited their own militia to protect their families and property. The land of the county was mainly in the hands of Anglo-Irish gentry, many of the estates having emerged from the plantations in the sixteenth and seventeenth centuries or being controlled by descendants of Cromwellian soldiers. Other estates had been granted to new English landlords as a reward for service to the Crown or the Church.

Some of Co. Wicklow's towns and villages were either created or remodelled by the gentry. Blessington, established under the Downshire family, is an example of an estate town. Edward Stratford, Earl of Aldborough, had an ambition to own a village that would carry his name. He noticed the ideal site high above the banks of the River Slaney in west Wicklow. The village of Stratford was thus conceived and named for his family, who had originally lived in Stratford-upon-Avon, Warwickshire. Stratford laid out streets and squares, built houses, and arranged a public lighting system. He also established linen and cotton industries, giving employment to a large number of local people. He proved his ecumenical outlook by building three churches–Protestant, Catholic, and Presbyterian.

The Fitzwilliams, Brabazons, Parnells, Wingfields, and Probys were among the other leading landlords, with large mansions and extensive estates throughout the county. Many were absentee landlords, opting to reside in their Dublin or London properties, where they had easier access to the fashionable circles of the period. The Fitzwilliam family in Coolattin owned the largest estate in the county, between Tinahely and Shillelagh. Fitzwilliam employed hundreds of local workers on his estate, to whom he was most sympathetic, assisting them in time of famine and need. His property in England was more extensive, and it was there that he mainly lived.

The principal estate in Greystones and Delgany was that of the La Touche banking family. In Arklow the Butlers leased most of their property in the district to Ralph Howard, who rebuilt the old Shelton Abbey in a gothic design. In the late eighteenth century Francis Synge took possession of 4,000 acres (1,600 hectares) of demesne that included the Devil's Glen and Roundwood Park. In 1804 he built a mansion called Glanmore Castle, designed by Francis Johnson. The property passed to his son, John, and on his death to John Hatch Synge, father of the playwright John Millington Synge. By then the estate had incurred huge debts and was greatly diminished. John Synge senior, a barrister, died when John Millington Synge was only a year old.

By the late nineteenth century the main landlords in Co. Wicklow were Fitzwilliam at Coolattin, Wingfield (Viscount Powerscourt) at Enniskerry, Brabazon (Earl of Meath) at Kilruddery, Monck at Charleville, Hodgson at Hollybrook, Leeson (Earl of Milltown) at Russborough, Ball at Newcourt, Parnell at Rathdrum, Hill (Marquis of Downshire) at Blessington, Beresford at Stratford, Howard at Arklow, La Touche at Delgany, Byrne at Croneybyrne, and Synge at Glanmore.

It was the landed families who dominated local administration for the 250 years after the Cromwellian settlement. The county sheriff was charged with the administration of the county, assisted by the grand jury. This was not an elected body but was selected by the sheriff from people of influence and wealth, and their decisions often reflected their political allegiance. They regularly presented addresses of loyalty to the monarch, to the displeasure of local nationalists. The grand juries were allocated responsibility for the construction of roads and other works.

They also assumed responsibility for piers, fever hospitals, county infirmaries, mental asylums, jails, and courthouses.

The Local Government (Ireland) Act (1898) provided for the introduction of the modern local government system. Local authorities, including Wicklow County Council, were established to provide and regulate a range of public services, and the county administration in Wicklow was placed on a representative basis. The establishment of local authorities in the towns of Wicklow, Bray, and Arklow at the end of the nineteenth century finally afforded ordinary people an opportunity to participate in municipal government. The first election, in 1899, returned seventeen nationalist and three unionist councillors from the electoral divisions. Among the first county councillors were veterans of the Land War and members of Parnell's Irish Party.

Until 1914 elections were held every three years. Simple majorities in the various electoral divisions decided the outcome. Under this new system of local administration Wicklow County Council was responsible for collecting rates, for the repair and maintenance of roads and public buildings, and for preparing the electoral lists for the county.

7 INDUSTRIES

GOLDMINING

FROM THE STONE AGE there had been finds of gold in the rivers and mines of Co. Wicklow; but in the late eighteenth century a gold rush occurred in the Woodenbridge area. The main source of the find was the Gold Mine River, where a fisherman discovered gold and worked it profitably for twelve years. It was only when a local boy, John Byrne, discovered a gold nugget that the river was panned extensively. Several other finds were made, and in 1795, when this became public knowledge, gold fever set in.

Within weeks, hundreds of ill-clad prospectors besieged the area in search of their fortune. Local landlords were incensed by their activities and protested to the government that they could not recruit labourers to gather the harvest. The government took possession of the mine, and the Kildare Militia was despatched to patrol the river. In 1797 an act of Parliament was passed under which the Gold Mining Company began operations, and large quantities of ore were found. Nuggets weighing between $2\frac{1}{2}$ and 18 ounces (70–500 grams) were found; in all, some 2,666 ounces (75 kilograms) of gold were discovered.

AVOCA MINES

Avoca has had a long association with the mining industry from ancient times, particularly in the Cronebane area. In the twelfth century there was a report that two of Strongbow's knights worked iron mines in the area. In the early eighteenth century Matthew Johnson discovered a rich copper vein, and within two decades several smelting works had been established. In 1780 one of the largest mine-owners was John Howard Kyan, who began smelting the ore. In the early nineteenth century steam power replaced the horse and waterwheel as the main source of power at the mines. The Railway Commissioners' map of Ireland (1837) showed several mining areas in Co. Wicklow.

Up to 1839, Sicily was the main source of brimstone, used by the growing chemical industry in England for the manufacture of sulphuric acid, needed by refiners, die-makers, and tin-platers. A disagreement between England and the King of Naples led to a considerable rise in the value of sulphur. A search began for another source of raw material, which led to the Vale of Arklow. Avoca became established as the source of sulphur for the English chemical industry, based around Runcorn, Cheshire. Production at the Avoca Mines was quickly revived, as they had ample supplies of the raw material. Between five hundred and a thousand carts of ore were transported from the mines to the harbours at Arklow and Wicklow, and vessels were hired to transfer the ore to Dublin for shipment to the smelting-houses in Swansea.

Coal was imported from Britain through Arklow to power the steam engines scattered throughout the Avoca valley at the ore mines. In 1847, when famine struck, many carters became ill or died, leaving the ore to accumulate. Henry Hodgson, who had responsibility for transporting the ore, leased a strip of land from Avoca to Arklow and laid a railway line, which became known as the Mineral Tramway. Carriages were drawn by oxen, horses, and finally steam engines. The railway continued in operation until the Dublin and South-Eastern Railway came into being in 1856.

During the winter months many of the fishing boats were used to transport the ore to Dublin for shipping abroad. One side effect of the mining was the widespread killing of salmon and other fish in local rivers and streams.

The majority of miners lived in a *bothán* or one-roomed dwelling. The next step up was a two-roomed house, often shared by more than one family. Some of the workers lived in squalor, with poor sanitary conditions. Employment reached its peak about 1850, when two thousand miners produced 140,000 tons of ore. The mining company received 25 shillings a ton for the ore on the quay at Wicklow; the miners received 4s 6d per ton for raising it, and carriage to Wicklow cost 5 shillings per ton.

During a serious outbreak of cholera in Arklow, hundreds of victims died, while in Avoca there was not a single death, as sulphur was regarded as being the best disinfectant.

By the late 1850s the Catholic population of the parish of Avoca had reached 3,320. With the growing mining population it was necessary to build a larger church, to which the miners contributed generously, and in 1860 the foundation stone was laid.

By 1880 there was a drastic decline in the mining industry, as orders dwindled, followed by widespread lay-offs. Many of those working in the mines had come from England and Wales. When the mines closed, entire families returned home, leaving the area virtually derelict.

In the early years of the nineteenth century the Royal Irish Mining Company operated the lead mine near Drumgoff Barracks. At about this time mines above Glendalough were also worked, producing lead, zinc, and silver.

The BYRNES OF CRONEYBYRNE

The only large Catholic landlords in the county at this time were the Byrnes of Croneybyrne, who employed forty workers on their 3,000-acre (1,200-hectare) estate. Workers also came from Clara, Rathdrum, and Roundwood to process timber in the estate's sawmills. The Byrnes owned large tanneries in Liverpool, which required copious quantities of bark for the dyeing and tanning process. The bark from the beech trees of Croneybyrne was transported through the port of Wicklow for shipment to Liverpool, giving consequential employment to carters and shipowners throughout the county.

FARMING

Co. Wicklow is associated more with agriculture and tourism than with any other economic activity. Unfortunately, the numbers engaged in farming have dropped substantially in the past number of years due to EU agriculture directives. In the 1981 Census of Agriculture there were 3,306 farmers in the county with more than 15 acres (6 hectares). A decade later there were 2,730 holdings; of these, 2,691 were bigger than 2.37 acres (1 hectare) and 2,202 were bigger than 25 acres (10 hectares). The 1991 census also showed that the average farm size in Co. Wicklow was 126 acres (51 hectares). According to the census, 2,034 farms in Co. Wicklow had farming as the sole occupation, while 667 had additional income from other sources. A recent study by the National University of Ireland, Dublin, showed that up to 60 per cent of farm households had other income.

A report by Teagasc in 1999 produced some interesting facts. Approximately two thousand farmers in the county were employed in a drystock enterprise. More than 1,382 were engaged in cattle farming, with a total stock of more than 130,000. Up to 1,600 farmers had sheep flocks, and in 1996 more than 300,000 ewes were registered. There were 300 farms engaged in dairy farming. Approximately 25,000 cows contributed to the production of 25 million gallons of milk. About 12 per cent of the land, mainly in the east of the county, was suitable for intensive cereal-growing. The 600 farmers on arable land had approximately 360,000 acres (145,000 hectares) under spring barley and wheat and a further 106,000 acres (43,000 hectares) under winter wheat and barley.

In the past two decades, young people have been leaving rural Ireland in large numbers to work in information technology, industry, and construction, the higher incomes and access to social centres attracting them to life in the city. Farmers have found it necessary to augment their falling incomes with various alternatives. Some have diversified into 'agri-tourism', such as farmhouse holidays and open farms; others have invested in the renovation of outhouses as self-catering units. The mountainous terrain is also suitable for quad bike racing, mini-golf courses, adventure parks, forestry, and other enterprises.

Forestry is the most important alternative land use in Co. Wicklow. The Irish climate is conducive to the growth of trees. The lack of prolonged winter frosts makes possible year-round growth, and many imported varieties grow faster here than in their native habitat. So far, 93,000 acres (38,000 hectares), or 19 per cent of the county, is afforested, compared with 9 per cent for the rest of Ireland. The present grant system makes it an attractive proposition for farmers to plant trees, especially on marginal land. State-owned forestry accounts for 75,000 acres (30,000 hectares) and privately owned forests for 18,000 acres (7,000 hectares). The annual rate of planting in the county is now 670 acres (271 hectares) in state forests and 1,324 acres (536 hectares) in private forests. The harvesting and processing of timber, therefore, plays an important role in the economy of the county, with approximately thirty sawmills of varying size. The most important timber-processing firm is Woodfab in Aughrim, which employs 150 people and manufactures a significant quantity of processed timber and pulpwood.

Other uses of natural resources include the quarrying and preparation of the famous Wicklow granite at Enniskerry and Ballyknockan. Granite from Ballyknockan has been used in the building of the Bank of Ireland in College Green, Dublin, in Dún Laoghaire lighthouse, and in Liverpool Cathedral.

The outbreak of foot-and-mouth disease of 2001 had a damaging effect on many aspects of life and industry in Co. Wicklow, the consequences for tourism and agriculture being particularly serious. The price of sheep and beef fell dramatically, as people became wary of buying them; but with the passing of time, confidence has gradually begun to return to the beef industry.

8 The TOWNS

ARKLOW

ARKLOW (*An tInbhear Mór*, 'the great estuary') is a port and seaside resort in the south of Co. Wicklow near the border with Co. Wexford. In the sixth century St Dagán, a nephew of St Kevin, founded a monastery at Ennereilly, north of the town. The English name Arklow is of Norse origin (*Arnkel-ló*, 'Arnkel's meadow'), and the town was a Viking stronghold from the end of the eighth century.

In 1172 King Henry II of England granted the lands of Arklow to Theobold Walter, and it became the centre of power in the area. Walter built a castle there, and five years later he was appointed Chief Butler of Ireland. In 1285 Theobald Fitzwalter died at the castle and was buried in the convent of the Friars Preachers in the town. The castle later became the seat of the Butlers, Earls of Ormonde. In 1316 the O'Byrnes and the O'Tooles burned the town. In a subsequent battle the Earl of Birmingham defeated the Irish septs. Sir Anthony Lucy took possession of the castle and had it rebuilt and extended. With a reduction in hostilities the Butlers were able to return to the castle.

In 1599 the forces of the Earl of Essex won a battle against the O'Byrnes on the south bank of the river. In 1641 the O'Byrnes and

O'Tooles launched another attack on the castle, in which they wiped out the garrison. In 1649 the garrison burned the castle in an effort to impede Oliver Cromwell and his army on their march south. The same year many of the town's fishing-smacks were burned by the Irish to prevent the English capturing them. It is reputed that King James II stayed overnight in Arklow Castle after the Battle of the Boyne on his way to Waterford.

The Butlers leased most of the property in the town to Ralph Howard, who built Shelton House; in time his grandson was made Earl of Wicklow. In 1830 the distinguished architect Sir Richard Morrison rebuilt the house in gothic style. The mansion became known as Shelton Abbey; it now serves as a prison. In the adjoining Kilbride church, mausoleums have been erected for the Parnell and Howard families.

On the morning of 9 June 1798 a large force of United Irishmen left Gorey Hill for Arklow, where they faced a strong force of Redcoats equipped with cannons and muskets. The insurgents were poorly armed, with only an assortment of muskets and pikes. By mid-afternoon the conflict that became known as the Battle of Arklow had begun, and within an hour it had extended all over the town. Heavy fighting broke out in the area of the Fisheries, with its narrow streets of small thatched cabins, and the cabins were burned. Despite their lack of skill and equipment, the Irish fought with great courage, and after four hours they were in command. The army and yeomen were forced to retreat. Father Michael Murphy and seven hundred men were killed in the battle. A monument honouring Father Murphy and his men has been erected opposite the Catholic church. In 1799 the parish priest of Arklow was shot dead in his bed.

Arklow then was a fishing village, consisting of one long paved street of cabins and huts. Henry Inglis, in *Ireland in 1834*, described Arklow as

> *one of the poorest looking villages that could be seen. It is entirely supported by the herring fishing during season: but all the rest of the year is miserably off.*

From the early nineteenth century the diligent fishermen had cultivated a lucrative oyster fishery, and on many occasions oysters were exchanged for coal from England. In 1824 the first Arklow lifeboat station was opened, and since then the service has saved more than 330 lives. In the following decades Arklow was to develop into one of the most important maritime ports in the country. In 1865 it received a further boost to its prosperity with the opening of the Dublin–Wexford railway line. This and the success of the Avoca Copper Mines were two of the contributing factors in the growth of Arklow port. New piers were constructed, and there was a need for additional ships to export the large amount of ore excavated from the mines. Merchants in the town provided finance for building a fleet of ships, and offered fishermen shares to operate them. By the late 1870s up to eighty vessels were based in the harbour, making it the largest schooner port in the country, and its fleet of sailing-ships and schooners carried cargoes from Mediterranean and Atlantic ports.

In the mid-1840s Daniel O'Connell addressed a monster outdoor meeting on Catholic Emancipation in the Main Street. In 1858 construction began on St Mary and St Peter's (Catholic) Church. Dedicated in 1861, it is shaped like a Latin cross and is fashioned in the Grecian and Italian styles, without pillars. In 1899 St Saviour's (Church of Ireland) Church was built in the town in the early English style, embodying many features in churches of the shires of England.

The two world wars brought both prosperity and disaster to Arklow. The Kynoch explosives and munitions factory in Arklow operated between 1895 and 1919 and employed up to four thousand people during the First World War. It is reputed that during the war a German submarine attacked the factory. The remains of the submarine have been located on the Arklow Bank. Many merchant ships built and crewed by Wicklow men were lost in action in the Pacific and the Atlantic. The town was also noted for its building of boats and yachts. One of the best-known shipyards, that of John Tyrrell and Sons, built the sail training vessel *Asgard II* for the Naval Service. Tyrrell's also built the yacht *Gypsy Moth III* for Sir Francis Chichester, in which he won two transatlantic races. The town's maritime museum houses mementoes of many of these events and aspects of boatbuilding and the lifeboat service.

Arklow is still a popular seaside resort, with two fine beaches north and south of the estuary. The recent opening of the Arklow bypass has greatly relieved the town's chronic traffic congestion. The Nineteen Arches Bridge, which spans the Avoca River and divides the town, is the longest arched bridge in Ireland.

AVOCA

Avoca (*Abhóca*) is a picturesque village in south Wicklow, off the main Rathdrum–Woodenbridge road. The village was formerly called *An Droichead Nua*, Anglicised Newbridge, but eventually adopted a form of the name *Oboka*, given to a river-mouth on the second-century map by Ptolemy (Claudius Ptolemaeus), which shows a settlement corresponding approximately to the location of present-day Co. Wicklow. Originally the parish of Avoca was known as the parish of Redcross.

According to the Annals of the Four Masters, the fifth-century bishop Palladius built a wooden church at Teach na Rómhán, later called Tigroney, north of the village, said to have been the first Christian church built in Ireland. During the 1798 Rising the church was destroyed, and in 1803 the church at nearby Barranisky was completed. Castlemacadam, on the road between Avoca and Woodenbridge, derives its name from a castle destroyed by the O'Byrnes. In 1308 the Lieutenant of Ireland, Piers Gaveston, rebuilt it.

There is evidence that mining has been undertaken at Cronebane from an early age. A report in the twelfth century stated that two of Strongbow's knights operated iron works in the area. In the early eighteenth century Matthew Johnson discovered a rich vein of copper, and within two decades several smelting works had been established. From the middle of the nineteenth century there was an influx of miners into Avoca, who worked long hours in dangerous conditions for meagre wages, most of them living in a *bothán* or primitive hut. The prime years for copper-mining were the 1840s, when up to a thousand miners produced 140,000 tons of ore.

Avoca has been immortalised by Thomas Moore's melody 'The Meeting of the Waters.' In 1807 Moore visited the romantic setting and was inspired to write the famous poem while resting under an oak tree. Storms and floods have struck Moore's tree on several occasions, but it still stands today.

Another important feature of the district is Avoca Handweavers. The craft of handweaving in Avoca dates from 1723, with the traditional skills being passed from mother to daughter. The art of weaving played an important part in the lives of the local people, bringing them in extra income, and Avoca is now synonymous with high-quality tweed garments. In the 1990s Avoca became famous also as the fictional village of 'Ballykissangel' for the BBC television comedy series, filmed in many beauty spots in Co. Wicklow, including Enniskerry, Bray, and Powerscourt.

AUGHRIM

The neat village of Aughrim (*Eachroim*, 'horse ridge'), nine miles south-west of Rathdrum, is at the junction of several valleys, where two small rivers, the Ow and the Derrywater, meet to form the Aughrim River. To avoid confusion with the town of the same name in Co. Galway, the area was at one time known as *Eachroim Uí Bhroin* ('Aughrim of O'Byrne'). There is magnificent scenery along the valley of the Aughrim River, which extends north-west of Aughrim for ten miles to the foot of Lugnaquillia Mountain, the highest mountain in Co. Wicklow.

In the sixteenth and seventeenth centuries the heartland of the Aughrim country lay north of the village in the townland of Macreddin, sometimes known as Carysfort, after Henry Cary, Viscount Falkland. With the coming of the railway in the 1860s the centre of activity moved to Aughrim.

During the reign of Queen Elizabeth I the Lord Deputy of Ireland moved into the village when the O'Byrnes were subdued. King Charles I, later to fall victim to Oliver Cromwell, granted the rental of the two Sheenans (two townlands in the area) for the purpose of education in Carysfort. Once the Lord Deputy moved in, English settlers arrived and the population began to grow. In 1628 Carysfort was created a borough, with the right to send two members to the House of Commons. A school was built under the control of the 'Sovereign Burgesses and free Commons of the Borough of Carysfort.' In time this body disappeared, and the grant was administered by Trinity College and later by the Commissioners of Education until 1887, when the school was closed.

By 1798 Aughrim was a fully developed village, and it featured in an unusual incident on 20 September that year. The insurgent leader Joseph Holt, a gifted tactician, managed to draw the local commander, Hunter Gowan, and his forces out onto the Whaley Abbey Road. He then set the barracks on fire and burned everything belonging to Protestants (though a Protestant himself), which left him with a number of problems. His sister-in-law lived in the village, and he had difficulty saving her house. When he came to Michael Bolan's pub he was in a quandary, as Bolan had been a friend of his: if he left the house untouched it would be assumed that Bolan was in sympathy with the United Irishmen. So he instructed Bolan to break the pub's windows, so that it would be believed he had suffered during Holt's attack.

Anne Devlin was born at Cronebeg, Aughrim, in 1778, a niece of the insurgent leader Michael Dwyer and also of Hugh 'Vesty' Byrne. After her birth the family moved to a small farm at Corballis, Rathdrum. Anne's father was imprisoned for allegedly being 'very active in the rebellion,' and following his release in 1801 the family moved to Rathfarnham, Co. Dublin. All, apart from the youngest girl, were arrested and jailed.

Anne became involved in the rising and carried messages for Michael Dwyer. Robert Emmet employed her and her brother Arthur in his house in Butterfield Lane (now Butterfield Avenue), Rathfarnham. On 26 July 1803 she was seized by soldiers, subjected to the torture of half-hanging and pricked by bayonets in a fruitless attempt to force her to divulge the whereabouts of Emmet. She spent almost three years in different prisons, often in solitary confinement, and her health broke down. In 1806 there was a move to release all state prisoners, but the prison doctor, the notorious Dr Edward Trevor, managed to have Anne Devlin's name omitted from the list by moving her from Kilmainham to Dublin Castle. Her health deteriorated to such a degree that there was a petition to the new Chief Secretary, who agreed to her release. Recovering from illness, she worked as a housekeeper; she later married, but her husband died in 1845. Anne and her invalid daughter lived on the scant earnings of her son. She died in September 1851 in extreme poverty and was buried in Glasnevin Cemetery.

Patrick and Willie Pearse spent many summer holidays in the locality as children, as their uncle was married to an Aughrim woman.

North of Aughrim is Aughavanagh House, built in 1803 to guard the Military Road over the mountains. Charles Stewart Parnell later acquired the building as a shooting lodge. Later it became the country home of John Redmond, leader of the Irish Party in the British House of Commons. The building is now a hostel.

One of the biggest employers in the district has long been the state forest, where the variety of trees includes pine, larch, and fir. It supplied trees to the ESB, for the manufacture of paper for the newspaper industry, and for the building and hardboard industries. Aughrim was also noted

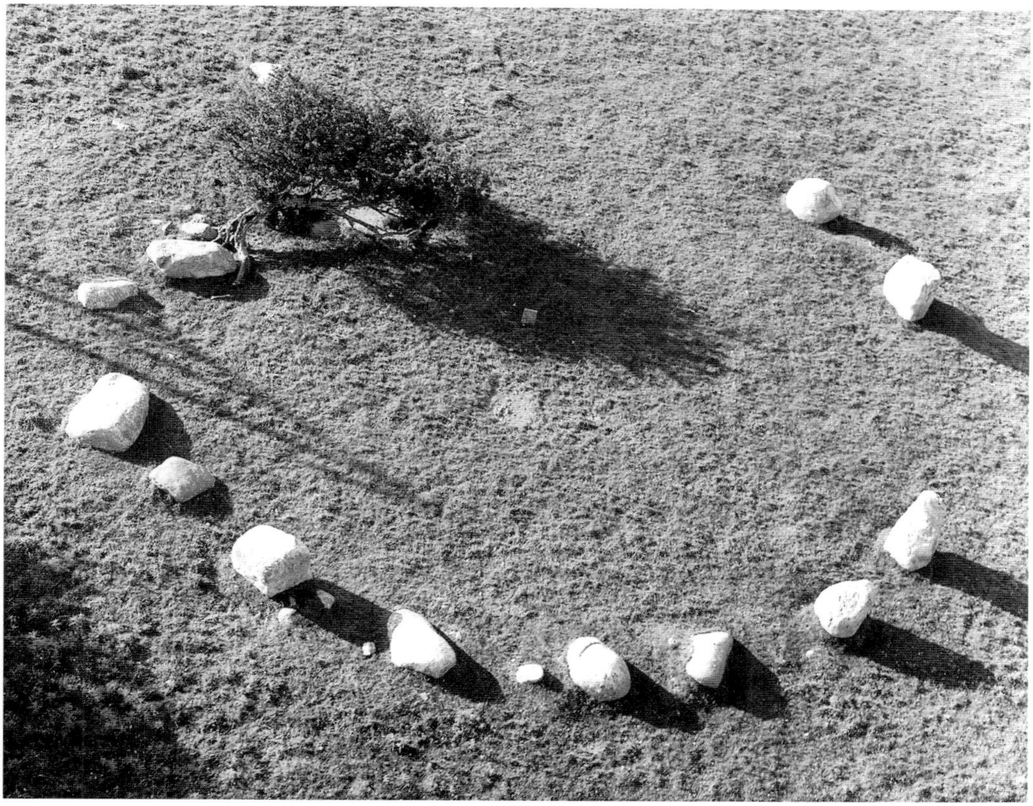

The Piper's Stones. This stone circle is situated at Athgreany on the Blessington road. (Dúchas)

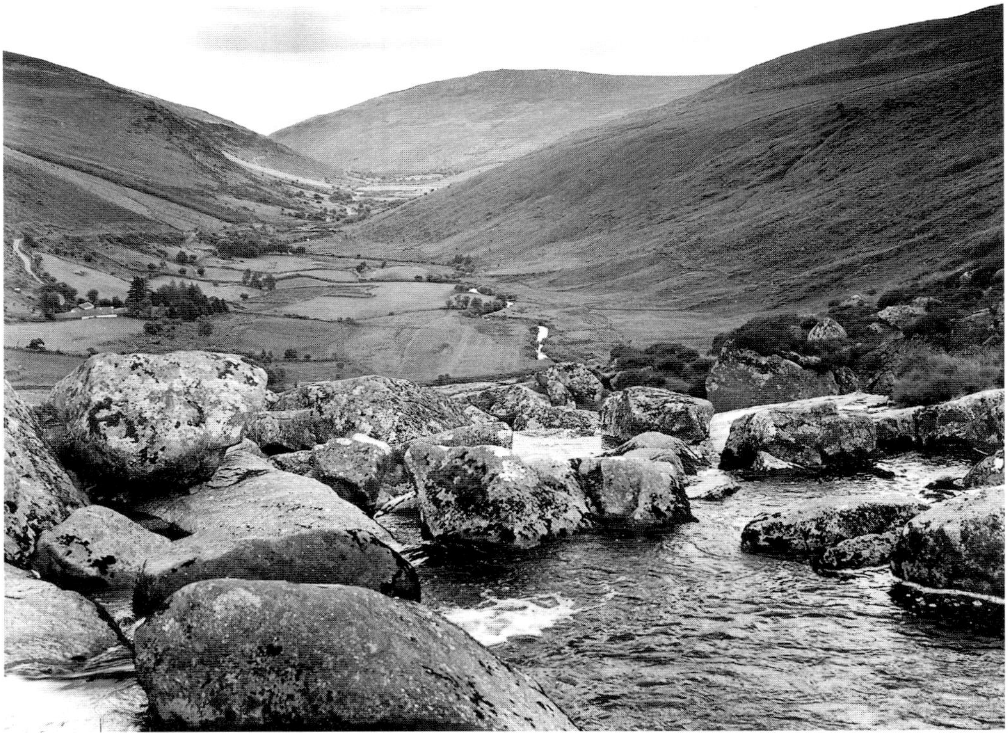

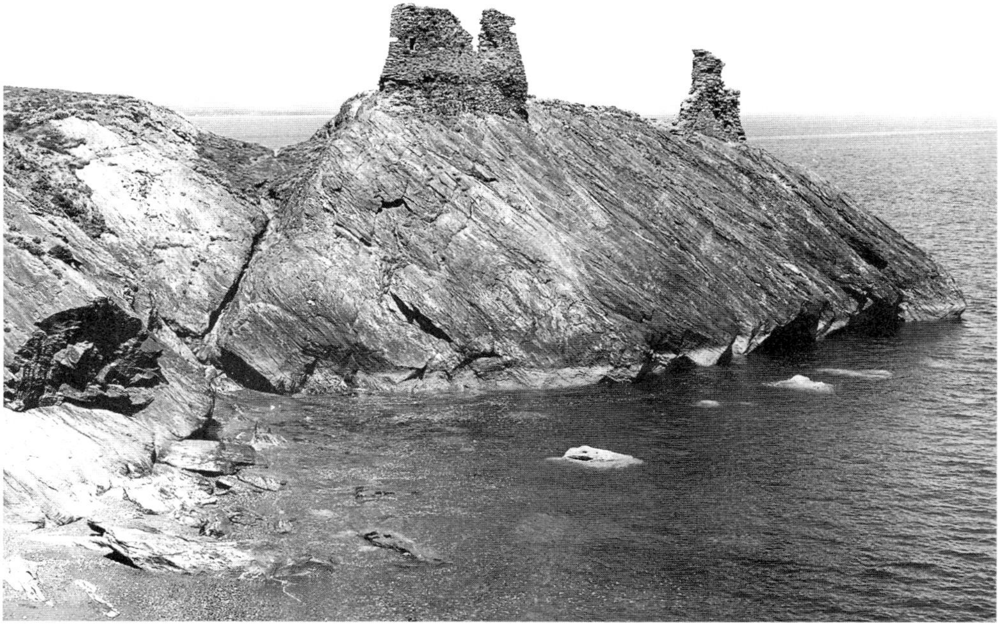

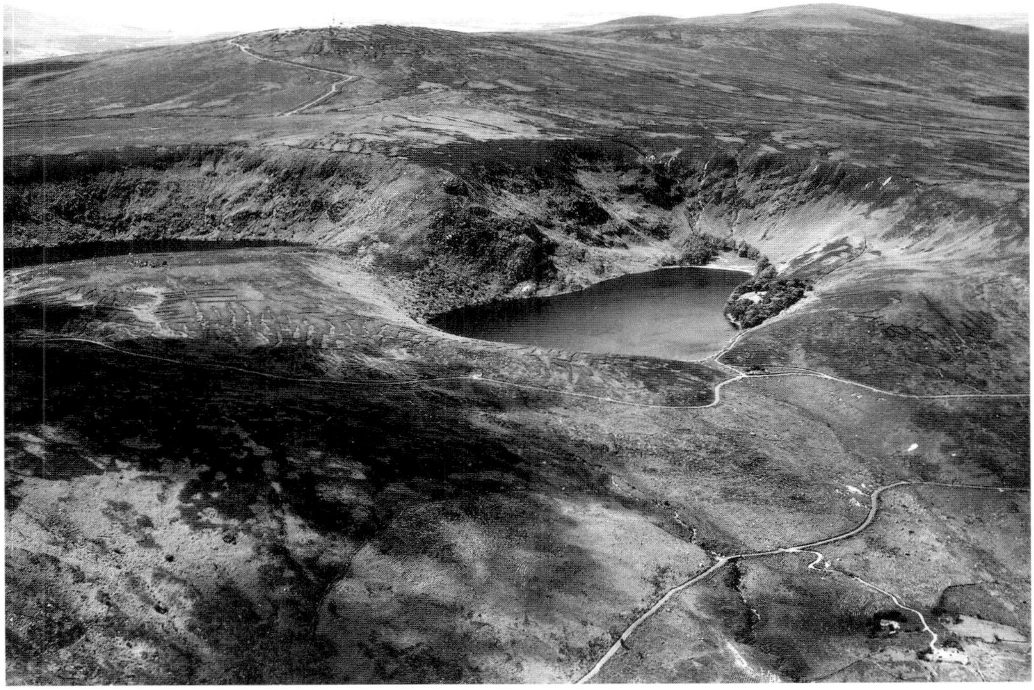

(*Above*) Aerial view of Lower and Upper Lough Bray, with Kippure Mountain in the background.

(*Opposite, top*) Glenmacnass. At this point on the road from Sally Gap to Laragh, the Avonmore river tumbles 80 m (262 ft) to the valley floor below. (Bord Fáilte)

(*Opposite, bottom*) The Black Castle was erected in 1169 on a rocky promontory over the sea close to Wicklow Harbour. The castle came under constant attacks from the O'Byrnes and the O'Tooles. (Dúchas)

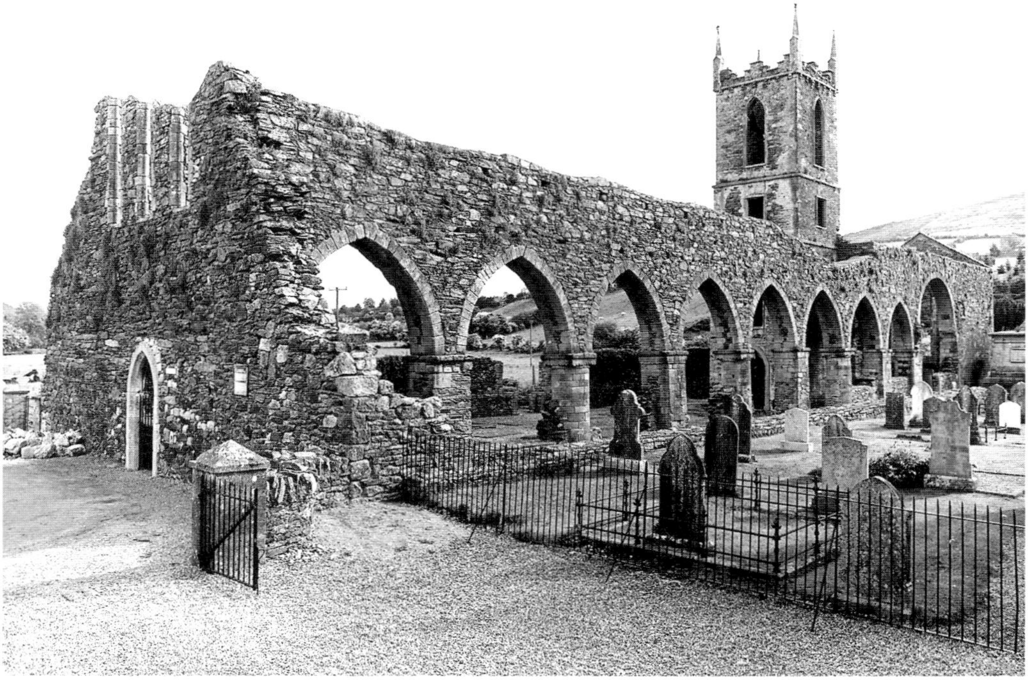

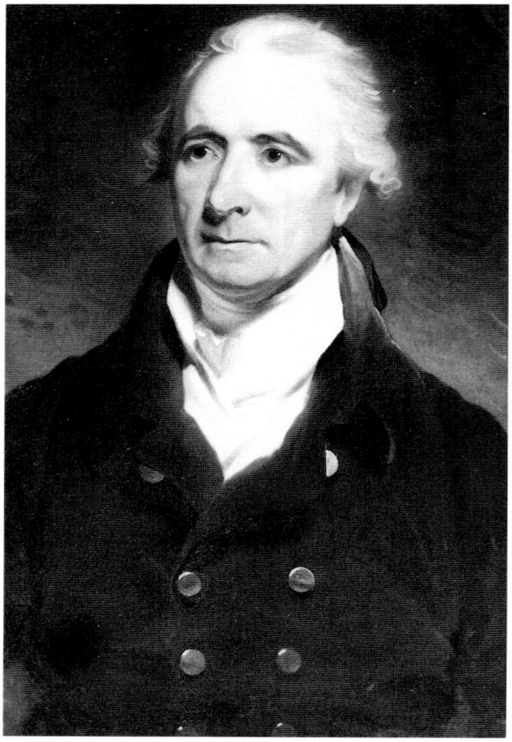

(*Above*) Baltinglass Abbey was built in 1148 by Dermot MacMurrough for the Cistercian Order. (Dúchas)

(*Left*) Henry Grattan (1746–1820), an advocate of legislative independence for the eighteenth-century Irish parliament, later abolished by the Act of Union. In 1784 he bought Tinnahinch House, near Enniskerry.

(*Opposite, top*) Killruddery House, Bray. Built in 1627 as the seat of the Earl of Meath. This photograph, c. 1902, shows one of the many lavish garden parties held in the grounds. (Lafayette Collection)

(*Opposite, bottom left*) Charles Stewart Parnell (1846–1891). Parnell was leader of the Home Rule movement and lobbied the House of Commons successfully for Land Reform. His relationship with a married woman, Katharine O'Shea, led to his downfall. (Illustrated London News)

(*Opposite, bottom right*) John Redmond (1856–1918). He was leader of the Irish Parliamentary Party who in 1914 called on the Irish Volunteers to join the British Army.

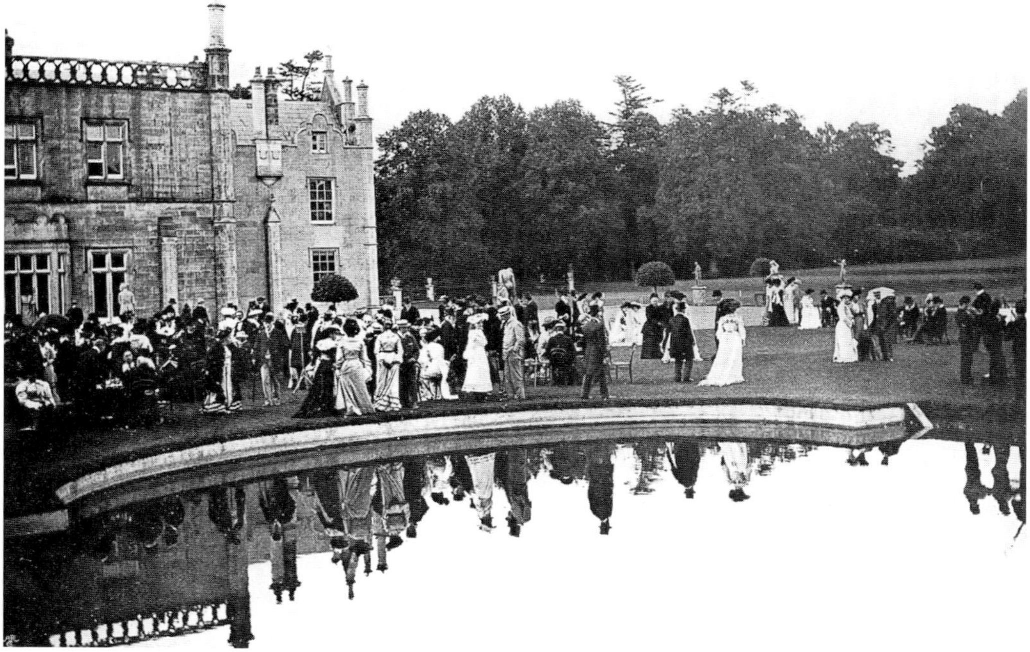

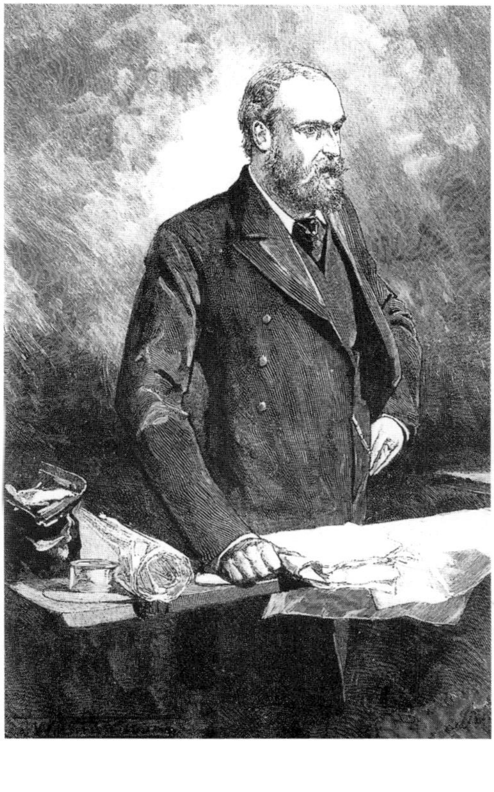

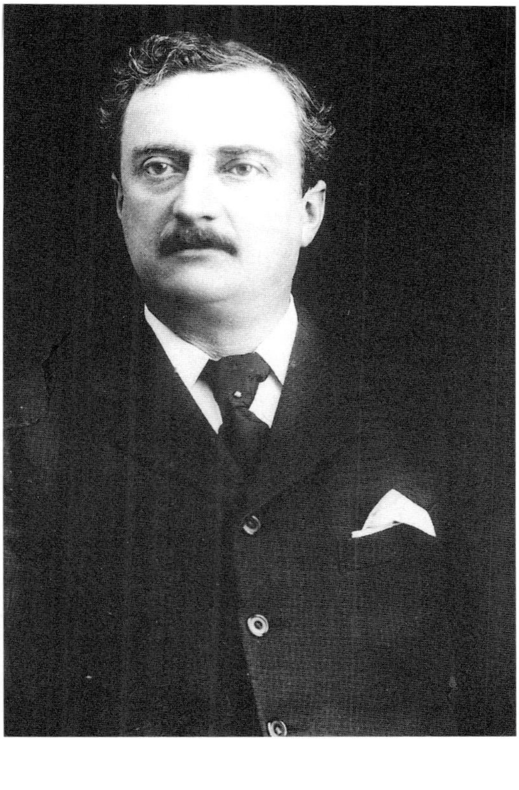

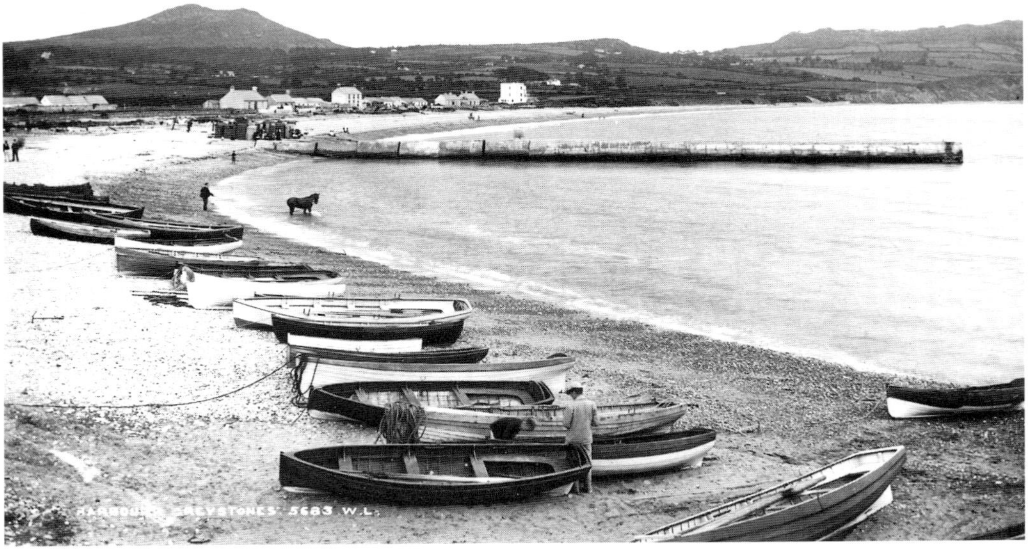

Greystones Harbour. A peaceful view of the small coastal town, c.1890. (Lawrence Collection, National Library of Ireland)

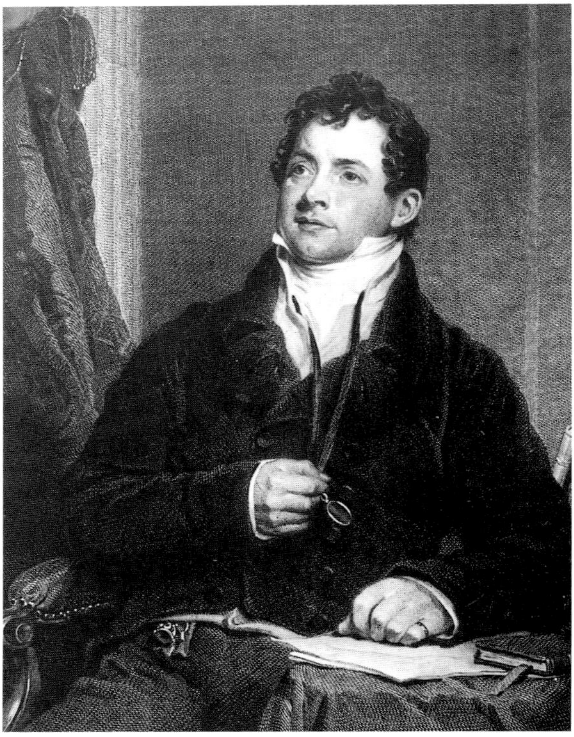

Thomas Moore (1779–1852). The well-known Irish poet and writer who published many works including *Irish Melodies*. (Hulton-Deutsch Collection)

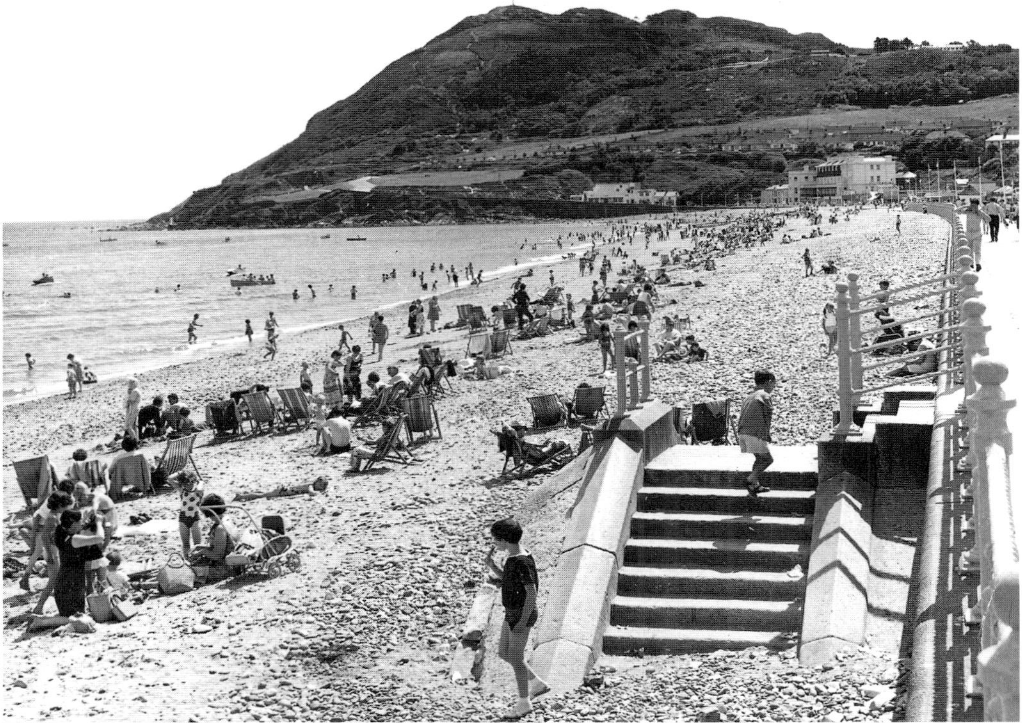

Bray seashore. Families enjoy a sunny day at the seaside. From the 1850s Bray was a favourite holiday destination. (Bord Fáilte)

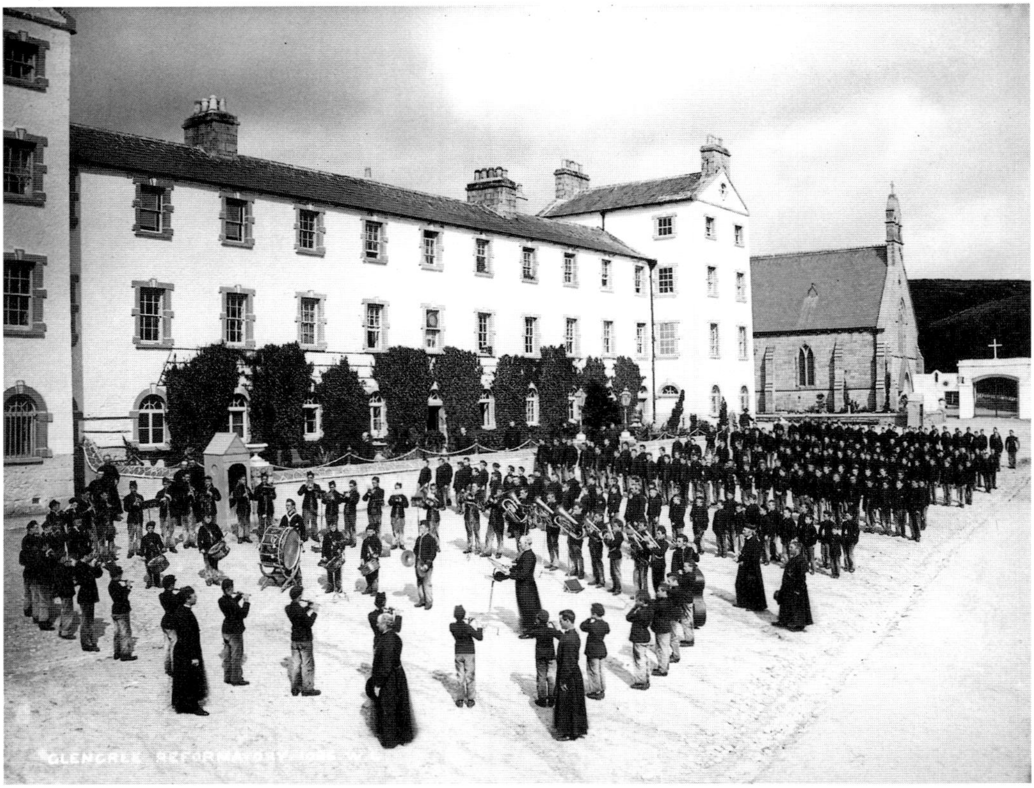

Glencree Reformatory (now the Glencree Centre for Reconciliation). Christian Brothers and boys parading in the yard of the reformatory, c. 1890. (Lawrence Collection, National Library of Ireland)

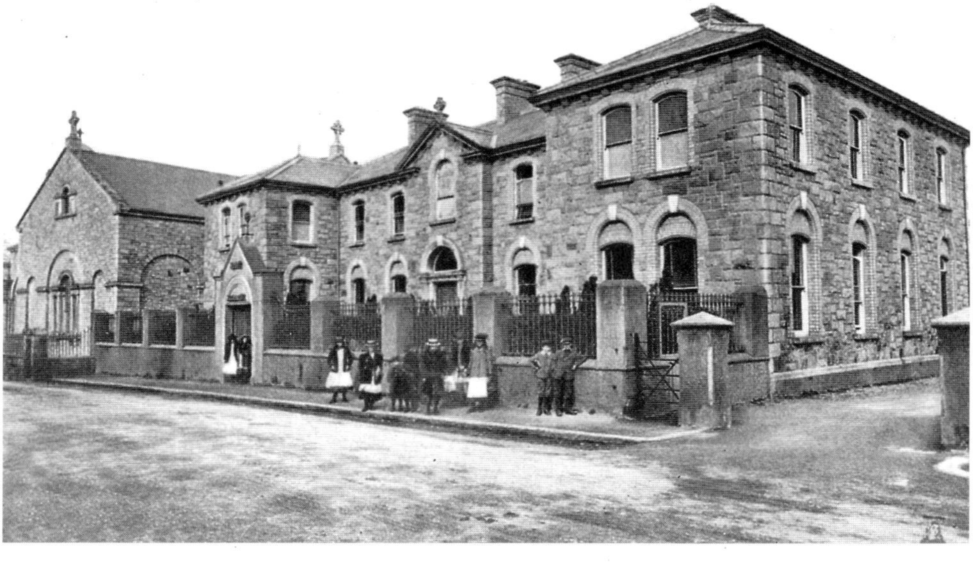

Arklow. Children outside St Mary's Convent, c. 1910.

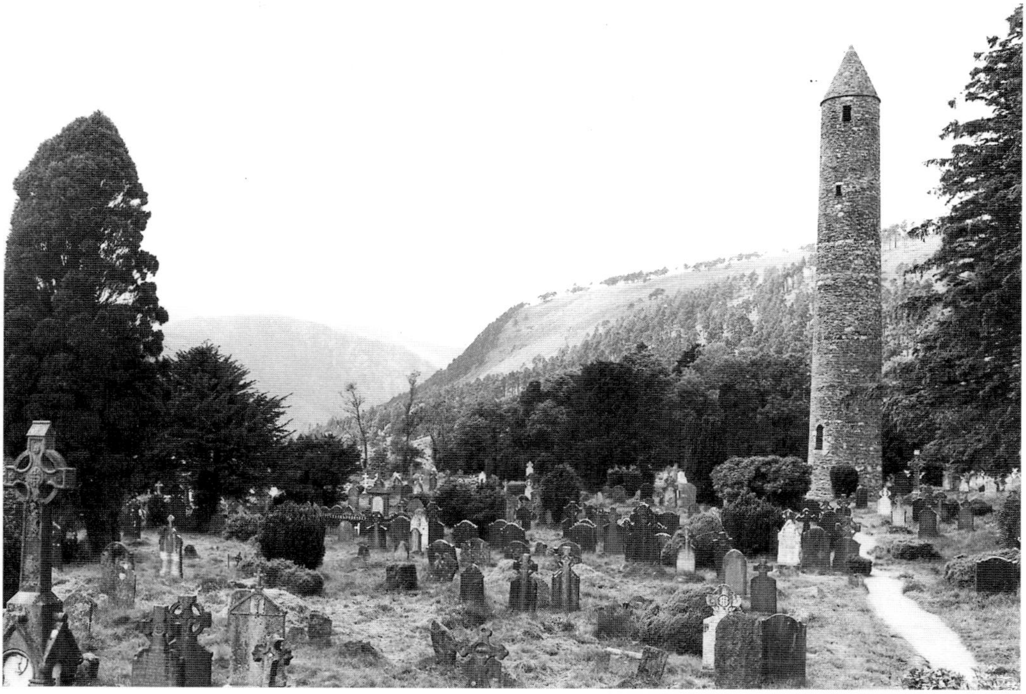

Glendalough with the Round Tower in the foreground. In the sixth century St Kevin founded a monastery here. (Dúchas)

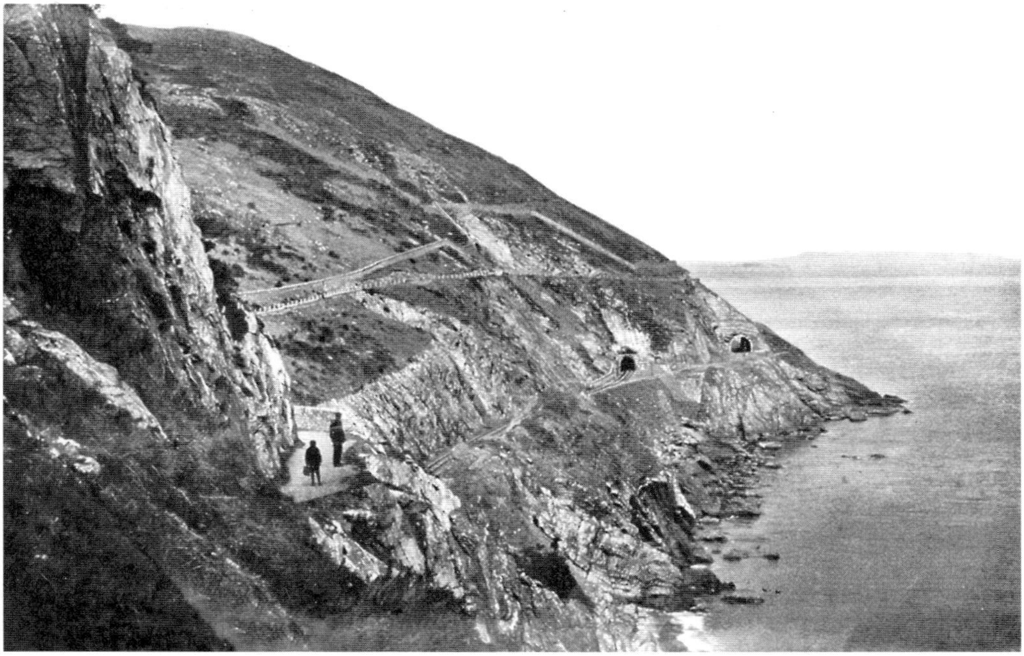

The Cliff Walk from Bray to Greystones, showing railway tunnels, c. 1907.

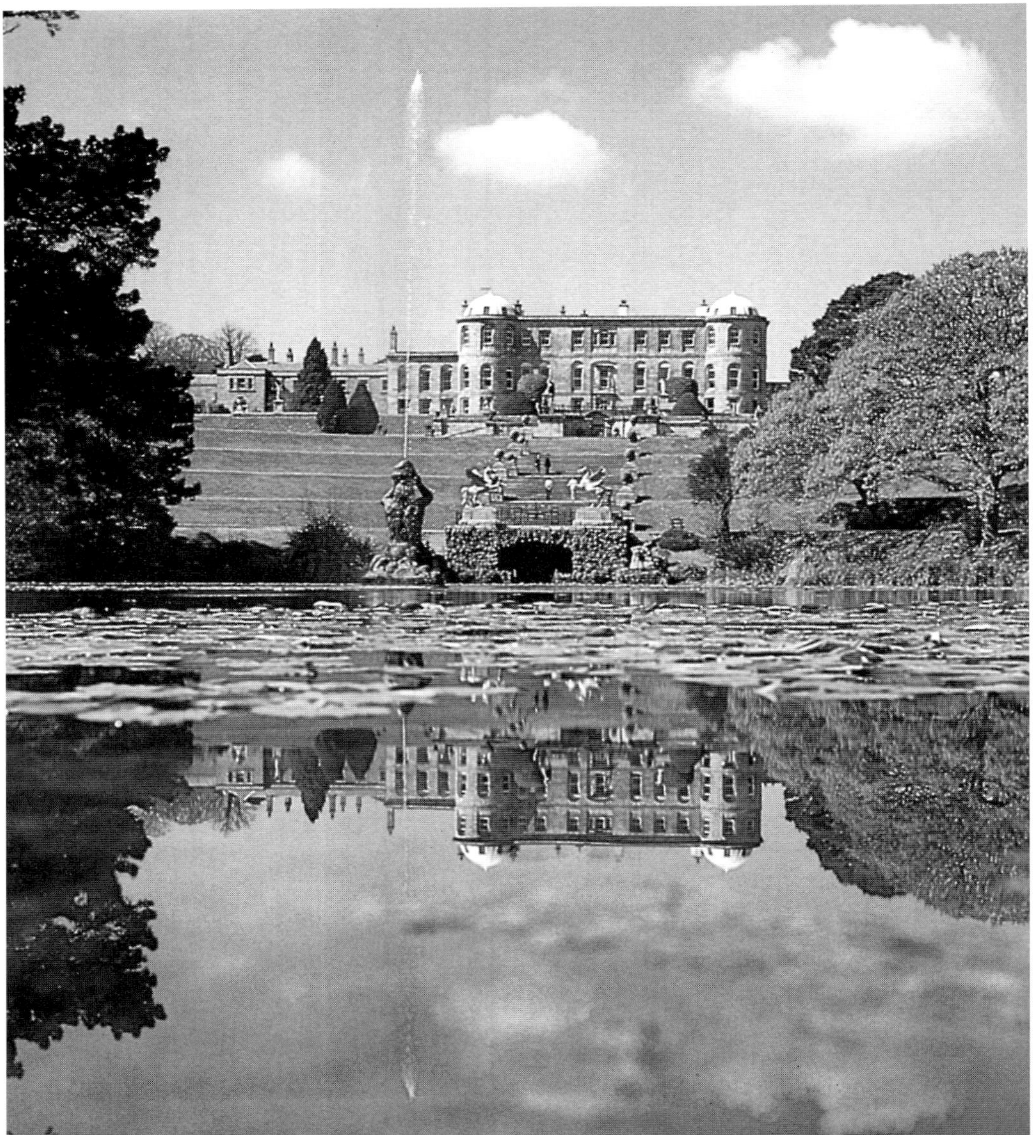

Powerscourt House and Gardens. In the 1740s Richard Wingfield laid out the elegant gardens of sweeping terraces, Italian statues and Japanese design. (Powerscourt Estate)

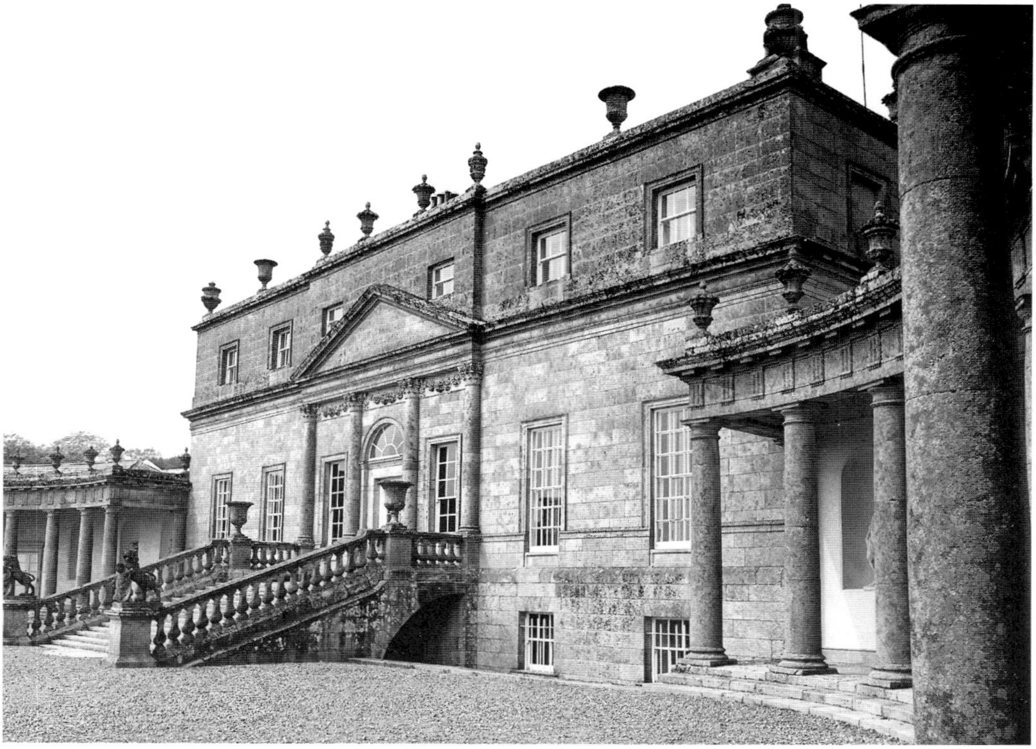

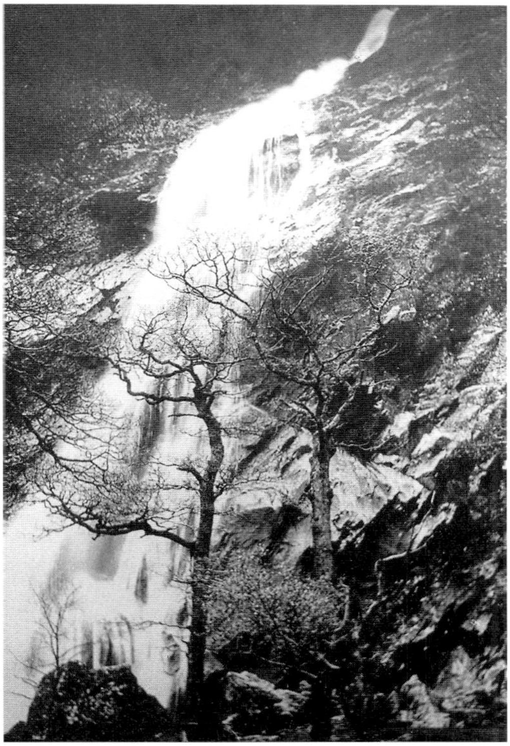

(*Above*) Russborough House, Blessington. Building of the house commenced in 1741. In 1952 Sir Alfred Beit bought the house and in 1976 he presented it to the nation. (Alfred Beit Foundation)

(*Left*) Powerscourt Waterfall. One of the most impressive features of the demesne is the 107-m (351-ft) waterfall.

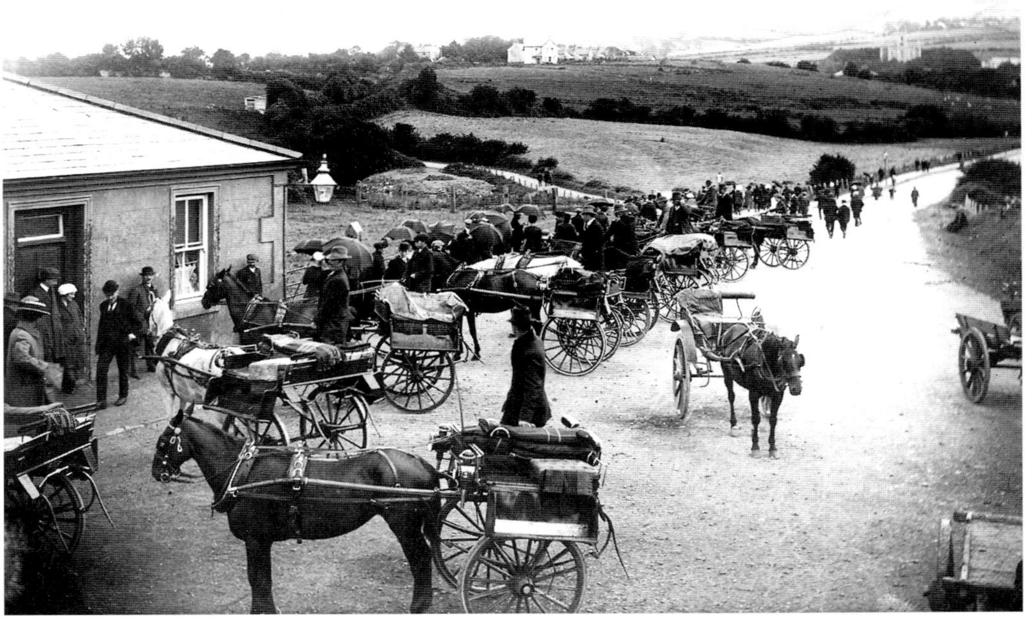

Rathdrum Station c. 1890. People and sidecars await the arrival of the Dublin train.
(Lawrence Collection, National Library of Ireland)

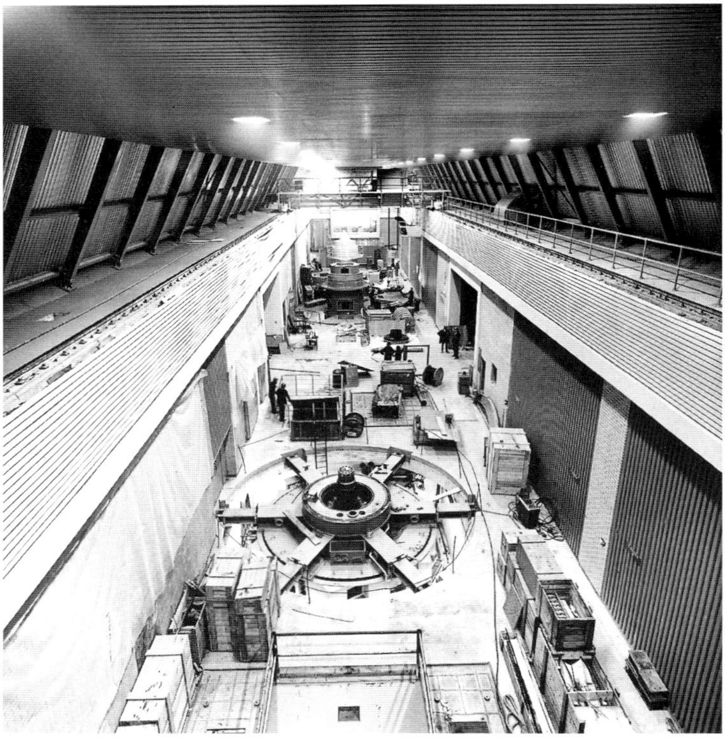

Turlough Hill. A view of the cavern in the ESB pumped storage station at Turlough Hill. (ESB Archives)

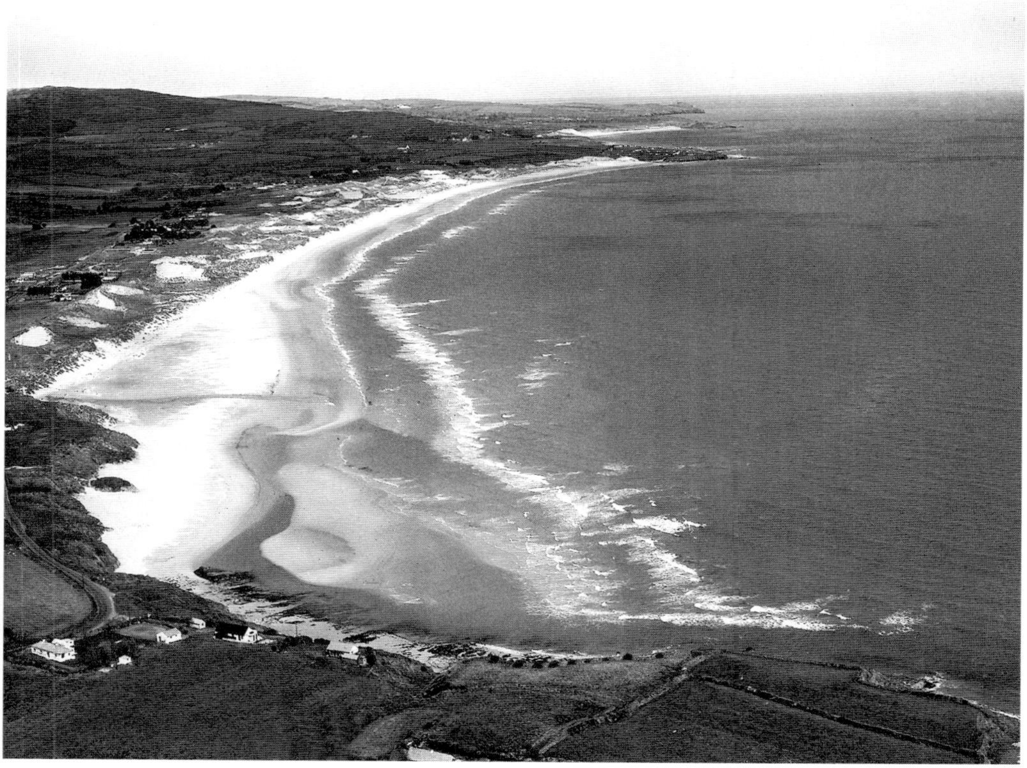

Brittas Bay. An aerial view of one of the finest beaches on the east coast with a 5-km (3-mile) stretch of white sandy beach and dunes. (Rex Roberts Studio)

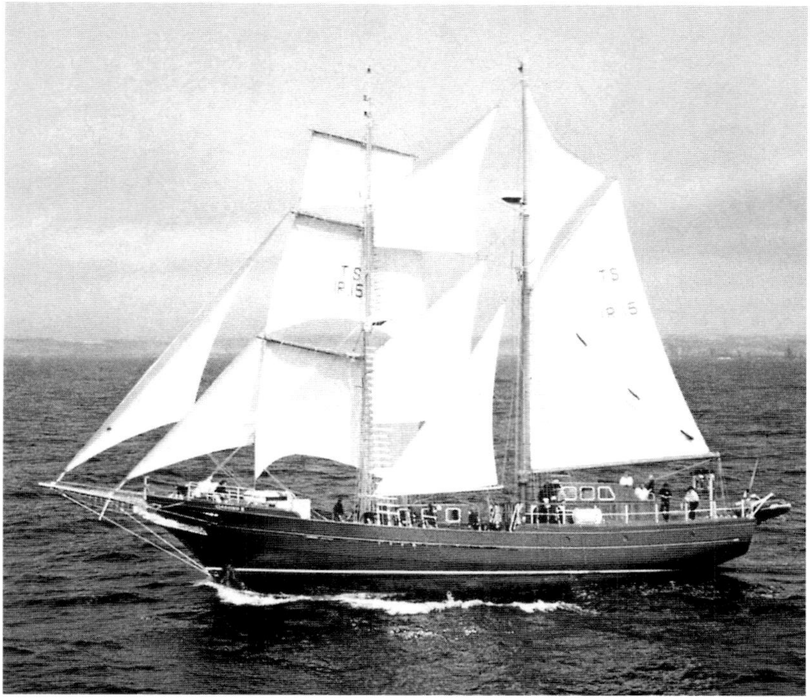

Asgard II. The well-known ship builders John Tyrrell and Sons of Arklow built the sail training vessel for the Naval Service.

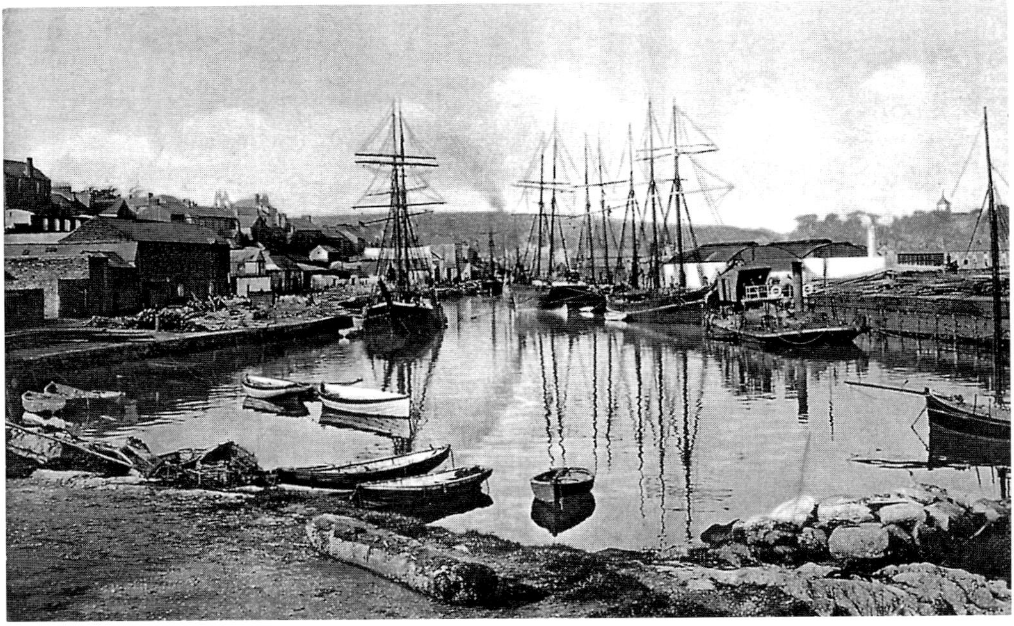

Wicklow Harbour. The busy quayside with sailing schooners, c. 1900.

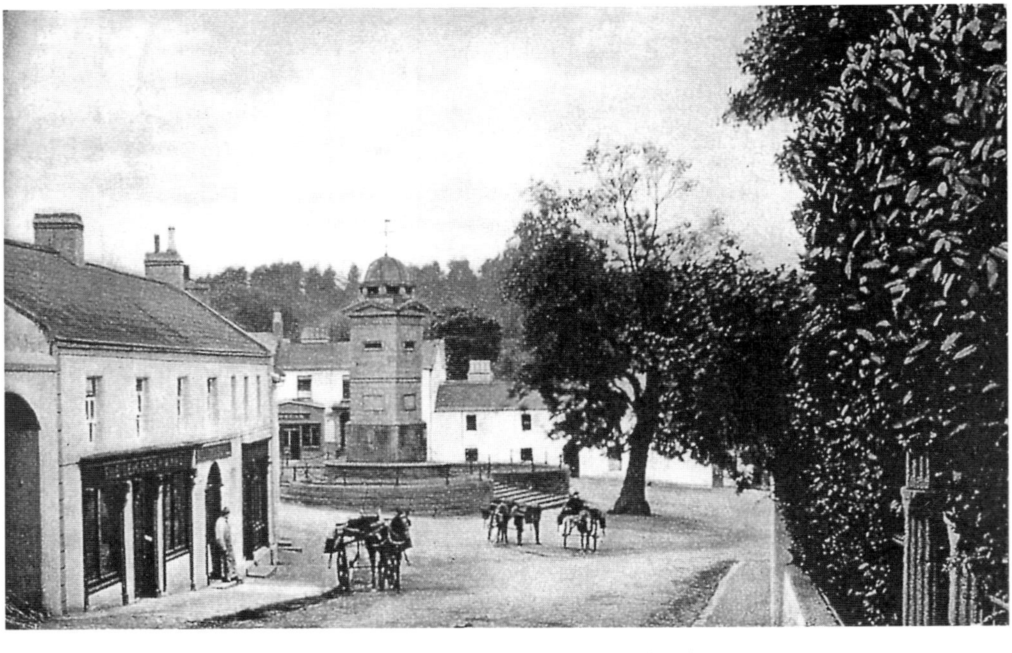

Enniskerry. The Main Street and clock tower with sidecars, c. 1920.

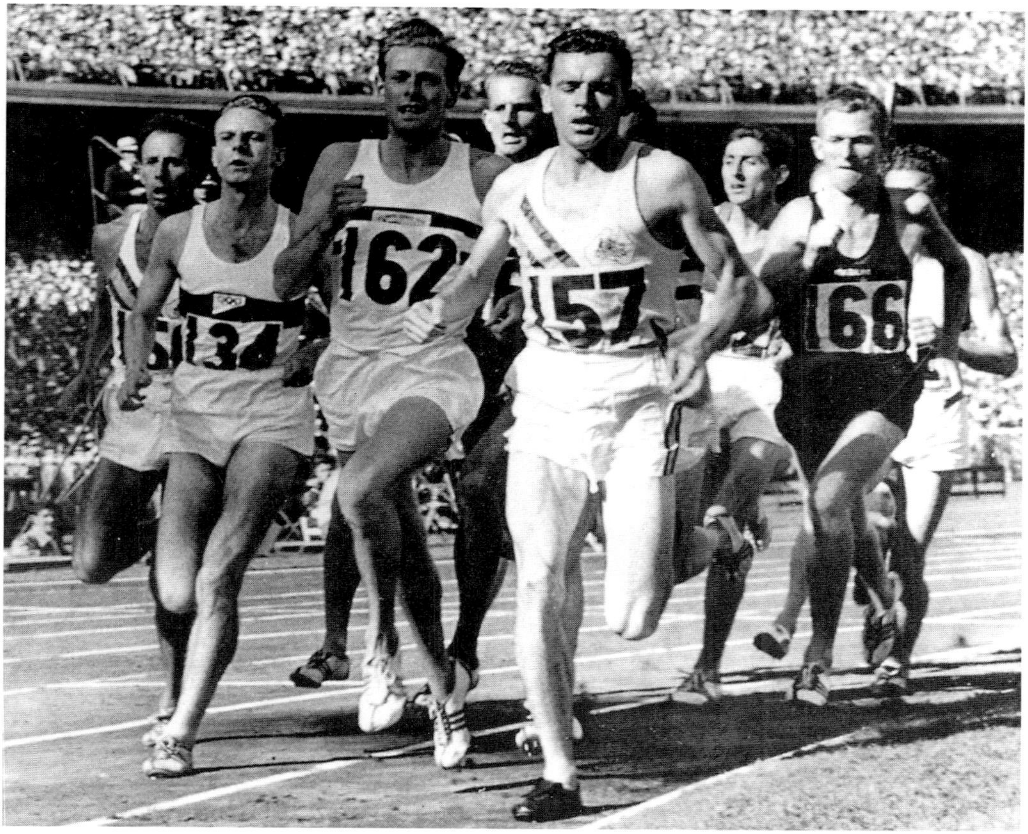

Ronnie Delany. The 21-year-old Arklow-born Delany (3rd from right) competing in the 1,500 metres at the 1956 Olympic Games in Melbourne, for which he won the gold medal.

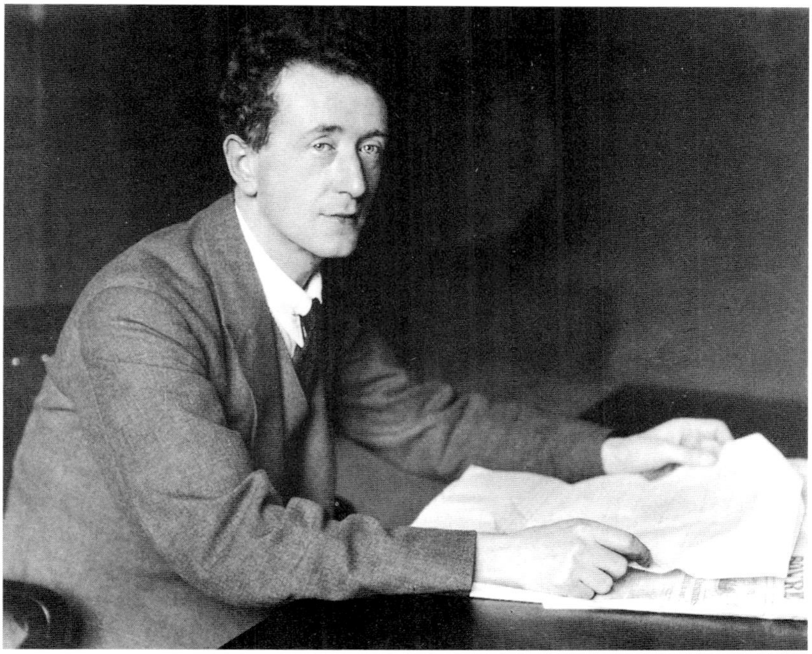

Desmond FitzGerald (1888–1947). He lived in Fairyhill House in Bray for many years, from 1914. In 1923 he became Minister for External Affairs in the Cumann na nGaedheal government.

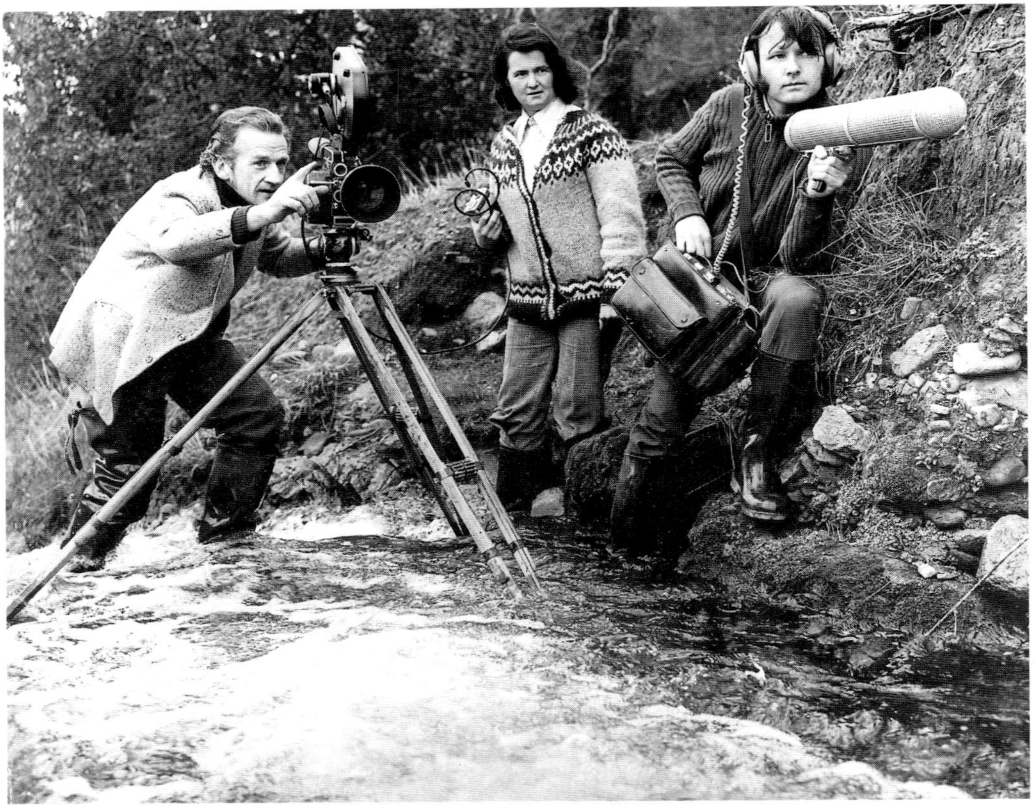

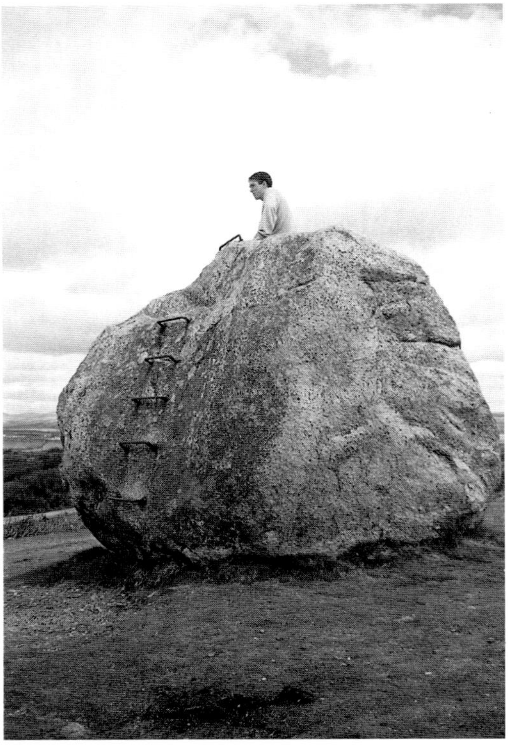

(*Above*) Éamon de Buitléar, c. 1965. The documentary and wild-life film maker, de Buitléar, filming on the Dargle River where he has lived for most of his life.

(*Left*) The Motte Stone at Avoca. This massive stone, weighing 100 tonnes, marks the site of a Neolithic settlement.

for its granite quarries, which in the early twentieth century employed up to a hundred men, and was sometimes referred to locally as 'Granite City'. Many of the older houses in the district are built from local granite. Granite from the Tinnakilly quarry was used in many churches in Dublin, and in 1934 the quarry supplied 450 tons of granite for the foundations of Liverpool Cathedral. It had hoped to receive the full contract, but policy difficulties led to the contract going to a company in Devon.

In 1996 Aughrim won the award of tidiest village in Co. Wicklow. A new amenity for the locality is a wildlife park and a four-acre lake stocked with trout. Aughrim has long been a strong GAA centre, and county finals are still played there.

BALTINGLASS

Baltinglass (*Bealach Conglais*, 'road of Cúglas') is a prosperous town on the banks of the River Slaney in the heart of west Wicklow. Baltinglass Hill is rich in archaeological remains, including a cairn and the remains of a passage grave and three burial chambers dating from the Bronze Age.

The town dates from 1148, when Dermot MacMurrough, King of Leinster, became interested in reform and built Baltinglass Abbey for the Cistercian Order and endowed it with eight separate grants of land. The abbey, known as Vallis Salutis, was one of the first to be occupied by the order after it arrived in Ireland, and the monks brought prosperity, agriculture, and industry to the community. They diverted the River Slaney and built a weir, corn mill, and woollen mill. In 1228 there were thirty-six monks and fifty lay brothers living in the abbey.

In 1397 the Irish Parliament sat in the abbey for three days. In later years the monks were accused of sheltering rebels, and with the suppression of the religious houses under King Henry VIII in the sixteenth century it ceased to operate as a religious centre. In 1541, following the dissolution of the monasteries, the eastern section of the church became the parish church. The ruins of Baltinglass Abbey include the nave and the base of two Romanesque doorways. Adjoining the abbey is a large pyramid-style granite mausoleum, built in 1832.

In 1617 King James I granted permission to Sir Thomas Willmott to organise markets and fairs in the town. In 1663 King Charles II granted an extension of these and granted a charter to the 'Sovereign, Burgesses, and Free Commons of the Borough of Baltinglass'. The corporation consisted of a sovereign (mayor), twelve burgesses, a recorder, a town clerk, a sergeant of the mace, and a clerk of the markets.

On 24 May 1798 an insurgent leader, Thomas Kavanagh, was betrayed and hanged in the town. On 23 February 1799 a party of eight men faced a court-martial for their part in the Battle of Derrynamuck the previous week. Captain McDonald, for the prosecution, alleged that the men had been members of Michael Dwyer's party in the battle. Two of the eight–John Ashe and Watt McDonald–were from Baltinglass. They were all put to death, with the exception of one man, who turned informer.

By the early nineteenth century Baltinglass had a population of 1,670 and was regarded as the capital of west Wicklow. It had a courthouse, a bridewell (jail), and an infantry barracks. The area had two members in the British Parliament, which ensured a good deal of funds and attention.

In 1840 James Frazer wrote about Baltinglass in his *Guide to County Wicklow*:

> *A poor struggling town, which though well situated as regards the surrounding district carries on little, if any, trade, the principal business being carried on in a few retail shops. There are, however, two bleach greens in the neighbourhood of the town.*

In 1950–51 Baltinglass made news when a dispute developed over the appointment of a postmaster. Helen Cooke had been deputising for her invalid aunt. The Minister for Posts and Telegraphs, James Everett, appointed a local man, Michael Farrell, instead of a member of the Cooke family. The appointment was bitterly opposed by the community; feelings ran high, and telegraph wires were cut. The dispute was finally resolved when the man appointed withdrew, and Helen Cooke took over the post held by her aunt for many years. The incident, which became known as the 'Battle of Baltinglass', was later the subject of a book and a television programme.

BLESSINGTON

Blessington (*Baile Coimín*, 'townland of Coimín'), the last Co. Wicklow town on the Baltinglass–Dublin road, existed long before many of the better-known settlements in the county. The English name Blessington, dating from the seventeenth century, derives from a mistranslation of the Irish name.

In 1667 King Charles II of England granted the area to the Archbishop of Dublin, Michael Boyle, who immediately set out to erect the Protestant church and other buildings and laid out a one-street village. He also built the impressive Downshire House, which was burned down during the 1798 Rising and never rebuilt. Boyle was also authorised to appoint a town clerk and town recorder to operate local courts.

About the year 1740 Joseph Leeson, son of a wealthy Dublin brewer and a member of Parliament, inherited his father's considerable fortune. He commissioned the German architect Richard Cassells to build Russborough House. It is built of granite in the Palladian style, of a central block with colonnades and two wings. Leeson was made Earl of Milltown and a member of the Privy Council. The house passed to his nephew, Sir Edmond Turton, who died in 1928.

In 1952 Sir Alfred Beit bought Russborough House as a home for his art collection. In 1976 he established a charitable and educational trust, the Alfred Beit Foundation, with the object of keeping the house and art collection intact. Russborough House has an excellent collection of art, dominated by Dutch, Flemish, and Spanish masterpieces and including silver, bronze, and porcelain. There were three infamous art thefts from Russborough House. The first occurred on 26 April 1974 when an IRA gang led by Dr Rose Dugdale took nineteen paintings; all were subsequently recovered. On 21 May 1986 the Dublin criminal Martin Cahill and his gang staged a robbery at Russborough House, in which they took eighteen of the most valuable paintings, including a Vermeer, a Goya, a Rubens, and a Gainsborough. In June 2001 a daylight robbery was staged at Russborough House in which two paintings, a Gainsborough and a Belletto, were stolen. Neither of these paintings has so far been recovered.

In 1840 Blessington had fifty houses, an RIC station, a hotel, and the extensive estate of the Marquis of Downshire. The borough of Blessington returned two members to the British Parliament. Mail cars bound for Kilkenny, Waterford and south-eastern towns passed through the town, giving it a new importance.

On 1 August 1888 one of Co. Wicklow's most famous transport systems, the Blessington tram, came into operation. The route first ran from Terenure to Blessington but was later extended to Poulaphouca; but the line came to be known as the 'longest graveyard in the world,' as there were so many accidents. Fatal accidents were marked by roadside graves. Nevertheless, the tram service continued until 31 December 1932, when it was replaced with a bus service.

On 18 April 1941, during the Second World War, four British airmen were returning from a raid on Berlin when their plane went off course and crashed into Black Hill, on the east side of the Blessington lakes. All were killed, and they were buried at the Church of St Mary the Virgin, Blessington.

BRAY

Bray (*Bré*, 'hill'), the most northerly town in Co. Wicklow, is situated on both sides of the estuary of the Dargle River. A primaeval forest north of the harbour has been radiocarbon-dated to 6,700 years ago. It was the town's strategic site at the mouth of the Dargle that attracted so many invaders to its shore. In 790 the Vikings established a small settlement here, from which they launched many raids on the monasteries of north Wicklow and south Dublin.

In 1171, as a reward for killing John the Mad, Strongbow granted the Norman warrior Walter de Ridelsford lands in Cos. Kildare, Dublin, and Wicklow. De Ridelsford built the great feudal Castle of Bré as a well-fortified outpost overlooking the river. The castle came under attack many times from the O'Byrnes and the O'Tooles; in 1310 they launched a successful attack and destroyed the castle. Edward de Boteler routed the attackers, and in the ensuing battle five hundred men were slain.

Close to de Ridelsford's castle a mill was built, where farmers could process their grain. A brewery and distillery were established nearby, and a small community developed around them. A barracks built in 1700 to help quell the activities of the rebel septs could accommodate two companies of soldiers. In 1818 the Earl of Meath bought the barracks and transformed it into a hospital. Close to the remains of the castle stands St Paul's Church, built in 1609. The original building was the Deanery of Bray during the Anglo-Norman invasion.

By the middle of the eighteenth century Bray was a medium-sized market town, with the poor living in deplorable conditions in mud cabins in Little Bray. In 1741, when the bridge was washed away in a flood, a sturdier one was constructed. In the later part of the eighteenth century Bray became associated with smuggling, as the concealed areas around Bray Head offered ample cover to the smugglers of brandy, tea, and silk. In 1804 the British, fearing an attack by the French, erected three martello towers along the coast, each one equipped with an eighteen-pounder gun and a small garrison.

The coming of the railway in 1854, combined with the nineteenth-century belief in the beneficial effects of sea-water, transformed Bray from a fishing town into a fashionable resort. Hotels and villas were built along the sea front and in the environs of the town, enticing such aristocrats as Sir William Wilde (father of Oscar) and Archbishop Plunkett to invest in property in the town. Quin's Hotel in the Main Street attracted the gentry and was a popular stopping-off point for coaches travelling between Cos. Dublin and Wicklow. An enterprising businessman, William Dargan, developed the town further, building the Turkish baths, Quinsborough Road and the promenade and earning the town the title of the Brighton of Ireland.

By the beginning of the twentieth century the population of Bray had risen to 7,500. One development was the demolition of a number of poor artisans' cabins in Little Bray and the erection of a hundred artisans' dwellings on the Commons, comprising Dargan Street, Maitland Street, and Ardee Street. On a number of occasions serious flooding affected Little Bray. In one disastrous flood on 26 August 1905 the river burst its banks; two thousand people, rendered homeless, were given refuge in various halls. The next building boom in Bray was in the 1930s, when many people from Little Bray were rehoused in new houses in Wolfe Tone Square.

One of the finest houses in the vicinity of Bray is Kilruddery House, home of the Brabazon family for more than four centuries. King Henry VIII of England granted the lands, once owned by monks, to the Brabazons in 1545, and in 1627 they were created Earls of Meath. In the Civil War of 1645 the house was destroyed, but it was rebuilt six years later. They were benevolent landlords and provided the town with a fever hospital, infirmary, town hall, and market house. Many roads in the town still bear witness to its loyalty to the British monarchy, with such names as Albert Avenue, Victoria Avenue, King Edward Road, and Prince of Wales Terrace.

Oscar Wilde came to the town on numerous occasions to visit his father's property in Strand Road. The writer James Joyce and his family lived at 1 Martello Terrace for four years from 1887, and aspects of the town featured in his later writing. Cearbhall Ó Dálaigh, later fifth President of Ireland, was born on 12 February 1911 at 85 Main Street. Others who lived in the town were the artist Paul Henry, the writers Sheridan Le Fanu, Philip Rooney, and James Plunkett, the conductor Hamilton Harty, and the politicians Desmond FitzGerald and his son Garret FitzGerald, Michael Woods, and Gemma Hussey.

In 1958 Ardmore Film Studios was opened, and during its chequered history many films were produced there, including *The Spy Who Came In from the Cold* (1965) with Richard Burton, *The Lion in Winter* (1968) with Katharine Hepburn, *Excalibur* (1981) with Nicol Williamson, *My Left Foot* (1989) with Daniel Day-Lewis, *Far and Away* (1992) with Tom Cruise, and *Braveheart* (1994) with Mel Gibson. In 1989 Neil Jordan filmed *The Miracle* on the sea-front and captured vividly the atmosphere of the resort. In 1997 John Boorman filmed *The General,* based on the life of the criminal Martin Cahill, on location in Bray, with Brendan Gleeson in the leading role.

Today Bray is primarily a dormitory town for commuters to Dublin. The once closely knit community, where sons and daughters have taken over family businesses, has been augmented by such an invasion of newcomers to the new housing estates that there has been a remarkable increase in the population since 1961. In the 1971 census the population of the town was 15,737. By 1981 it had increased to 22,853; by 1996 it had climbed to 25,252. In the 2002 census the total stood at 26,216. There has been considerable upgrading of the road system, with the Bray bypass saving valuable time on journeys from Dublin southwards, while the Southern Cross route provides a connection from the Bray–Greystones road to the N11. The town is also serviced by the DART (Dublin Area Rapid Transport) suburban railway, which links Bray with Dún Laoghaire, Dublin, and Howth.

CARNEW

The village of Carnew (*Carn an Bhua,* 'cairn of the victory') is close to the Co. Wexford border and forms the southern part of the barony of

Shillelagh. The dominant feature of the village is Carnew Castle, built in 1616 and now in private ownership. In 1649 Oliver Cromwell visited the area, and his soldiers attacked and destroyed the old castle. It was later rebuilt, and English soldiers were garrisoned there during the 1798 Rising. A rock above the village was known as 'Cromwell's Rock'.

In 1798 several battles were fought in and around the area. The reason for the turmoil was the memory of the massacre in Carnew ball alley on 25 May 1798. At the March assizes that year, sixty-one men were found not guilty of being rebels, but they were rearrested and imprisoned in the guardhouse of Carnew Castle. By direction of the local magistrate, forty-one of the prisoners were brought to the ball alley and shot. Miles Byrne in his memoirs describes it as the bloodiest deed ever recorded since the days of Cromwell. A force of United Irishmen who were camped at Kilcavan Hill set fire to the village in retaliation for the massacre. Thereafter Carnew came under fire from the insurgents, and there were attacks on the loyalist population and their property.

On 30 May 1798 Ballyellis, close to Carnew, was the scene of a battle when Joseph Holt led a force of United Irishmen from Cos. Wicklow and Wexford and encountered the Ancient Britons, a cavalry regiment, who were despised by the people. Most of the soldiers were slaughtered in the battle; there were no casualties on the insurgent side. The British government attempted to cover up the report of the deaths.

During the 1830s Carnew consisted of one street with a small brewery, two tobacco factories, a slate quarry, and a dispensary. Many of the women were employed in the spinning and weaving mills.

DELGANY

Delgany (*Deilgne*, 'thorny place') is a prosperous village set in a wooded area between Greystones and the N11 road. St Mochoroc, a Briton, is the saint most associated with the area. It is reputed that he established a church there and lived in a cell about the year 492. In 1021 the Hiberno-Norse King of Dublin, Sitric Mac Amhlaíbh, was defeated there in a battle with the Wicklow septs.

In 1753 the La Touche family came to Delgany. They were originally a family named Digges who left England during the reign of King Henry II and settled at La Touche, near Blois. They joined a Huguenot regiment that was fighting for William of Orange, and it was with that regiment that the first La Touche came to Ireland. David La Touche bought Ballydonagh estate in 1753 and built a house there; he later renamed it Bellevue. The family played a significant role in the development of the Delgany area.

There are two ancient castles in the district. The castle at Killincarrig was built in 1615. In 1649 forty Irishmen, defending English loyalists against English republicans, were garrisoned there. When Oliver Cromwell was leading his army from Dublin to Wexford the small garrison, under Captain O'Day, realising they could offer no resistance, retreated to Arklow. Cromwell rested there overnight before resuming his journey. An Anglo-Norman family, De Kenleye, from which the townland of Kindlestown was named, built the second castle in the area. In 1301 Albert de Kenly was Sheriff of Kildare.

In the early years of the nineteenth century the population of Delgany was just over two hundred. Among these were the members of the enclosed Carmelite order of nuns, who came to Delgany in 1844 and still live there. They provided education for local children, and it was not until 1892, when the Holy Faith nuns came to Greystones, that the Carmelites returned fully to the contemplative life.

ENNISKERRY

The village of Enniskerry (*Áth na Sceire*, 'ford of the reef') lies in the basin formed by Cookstown, Monastery, and towering Kilgarron and is surrounded by hills and mountains. The name is first mentioned in 1668 and appears to refer to a ford where the old road crossed the Cookstown River. The portal tomb at Parknasilloge and the one at Onagh are evidence that the district was inhabited in the Bronze Age. To the north of Enniskerry is the Scalp, a deep, narrow gorge whose steep cliffs of granite boulders run parallel to the road. The distinctive features of the Scalp date from the Ice Age.

In the eighth century Dónall Mac Giolla Mocholmóg ruled the sept of Uí Dunchadha, which occupied Enniskerry and its environs. They had a settlement in Curtlestown, on the road to Glencree. The area was granted to members of the La Poer family (from which the name Powerscourt derives) when one of its daughters married Milo de Cogan, one of Strongbow's knights. Later the O'Byrnes and the O'Tooles evicted him, and Féilim Ó Tuathail remained in possession of the property until his death in 1603. The area was then granted to Sir Richard Wingfield, who became Viscount Powerscourt. He rebuilt the old castle and a church that became known as the parish of Stagonil.

The village of Enniskerry came into existence in the early 1820s, when the first buildings were erected. It was given its distinct identity when Viscount Powerscourt built the clock tower and many of the buildings. The other churches and some elegant valve towers were also erected at about this time. A proposal to build a railway line from Bray to Enniskerry was aborted.

A prominent figure with local connections was Henry Grattan. The Parliament voted £100,000 to him for his services to the Crown; in 1784 he accepted half the amount, with which he bought an old coaching inn at Tinnahinch and converted it into a mansion.

In 1943, at the height of the Second World War, Laurence Olivier chose Powerscourt demesne for the filming of the spectacular Battle of Agincourt scenes for *Henry V.* The 510 foot-soldiers and 164 horsemen required were recruited from the unemployed and members of the Local Defence Force. Enniskerry, with a population of 370, became a boom village for the duration of the filming and was unable to cope with the demand for supplies. Many other films have been shot in Powerscourt, including *Captain Lightfoot* (1955), *Images* (1972), *Barry Lyndon* (1975), *The Count of Monte Cristo* (1975), and *Excalibur* (1981).

Enniskerry and Powerscourt have two of the country's leading tourist attractions. One of the most impressive features is the waterfall, at 351 feet (107 metres) the highest in Ireland. During the nineteenth century the elegant gardens at Powerscourt House were laid out in the Italian style; in 1974 the house was destroyed by fire, but it has since been partly restored.

GLENDALOUGH

Glendalough (*Gleann Dá Loch,* 'valley of the two lakes') has contributed significantly to Co. Wicklow's reputation for historical and archaeological importance combined with primitive beauty. The famous monastery here was founded by St Kevin in the sixth century, and it quickly became one of the largest ecclesiastical settlements in Europe. From 795 onwards it was to suffer at the hands of the Viking invaders, who burned and plundered it on several occasions. In 1111, following the Synod of Ráth Bhreasail, Glendalough was designated one of the two sees of north Leinster. The monastery was later associated with Laurence O'Toole (Lorcán Ó Tuathail), who became abbot of Glendalough in 1157 and Archbishop of Dublin in 1161.

The mines above Glendalough were active during the nineteenth century, when lead, zinc, and silver were produced in large quantities. One mine was called Van Diemen's Mine, referring to the penal colony of Van Diemen's Land (Tasmania), because of its remote site and tough working conditions. Outlines of the horse-drawn tracks are still visible there.

For centuries the beauty and tranquillity of the area have attracted tourists in huge numbers. The Glendalough Visitors' Centre is a worthwhile stop for those wishing to familiarise themselves with the landscape and history of the area. The centre organises guided tours, exhibitions, and audiovisual presentations. There are also ecological tours of the Wicklow Mountains National Park led by biologists.

GREYSTONES

Greystones (*Na Clocha Liatha*) is a prosperous coastal town 5 miles (8 kilometres) from Bray, immediately south of Bray Head. The town gained its name from the large expanse of rocks extending into the sea south of the town. The story of the town is one of two ruling families, the fishing industry, and the arrival of the railway. The roots of the town's history were planted at Ennis's Lane, a mile north of the harbour. This was the site of Rathdown Castle, one of the strongholds of the owners of the territory of Rathdown. In 1536 the castle and lands were granted to Peter Talbot, a noted defender of the Pale. The arrival from France of the Huguenot banker David La Touche, who bought the Ballydonagh estate at Delgany in 1753, proved another incentive for the area, and the La Touche family was to play a leading role in the development of the town.

In 1801 Admiral Whitshed was ordered to build martello towers, at a time when the British feared a French invasion of Ireland. He married one of the Hawkins family, who owned land in Killincarrig. His son, Captain Vincent Whitshed, lived at the Farm House on the Burnaby Estate. When he died a daughter survived him; she married a swashbuckling character named Colonel Fred Burnaby of the 2nd Dragoon Guards, a politician, balloonist, and traveller and the author of *A Ride to Khiva* (1877). Harry St Vincent Burnaby followed, and the Whitshed Estate became the Burnaby Estate. The big houses gave a good deal of employment to the poor of the district.

In 1795 the magazine *Hibernia* described Greystones as a noted fishing village. According to Eugene O'Curry there was a church near the castle, and the area was associated with St Crispin, who was believed to have had a cell there. Rathdown was later granted to Richard Edwards, and in time it was transferred to the control of the La Touche and Burnaby families. In the early eighteenth century the castle fell into ruins, but the name is preserved in a present-day housing estate.

When the power and wealth disappeared from Rathdown, the people in the area turned to fishing as a way of living, and Greystones became noted as a fishing village. The possession of a fine natural harbour helped considerably and paved the way for the building of boats by local shipwrights.

Like so many other towns on the east coast, the coming of the railway in 1856 greatly helped the development of Greystones. The construction of the Bray–Greystones section was a feat of engineering for Isambard Kingdom Brunel, one of the world's leading engineers. The line ran along the sea cliffs and involved three tunnels and four wooden trestle viaducts. Because of various problems with coastal erosion, sharp curves, rock falls, and resulting accidents, four diversions had to be made over the next sixty-three years. The route of the railway around Bray Head, with all its problems, seemed a strange choice for Brunel; but the Earl of Meath did not want the railway going through his land at Kilruddery, and so he gave the land of the Bray Head route free of charge. It was originally intended to have a double track through Bray Head, but this did not materialise.

In 1867 a temporary church, known as the 'Iron Church', was erected in the town. Before this the priest had to travel from Bray on horseback over Windgates to say Mass in a hall every Sunday.

By 1910, when Frank Porter was researching his *Wicklow Directory*, Greystones had become a well-established town, with the Evans family much in evidence. In the early part of the century Michael Collins paid many visits to the town to the de Valera family, who were living there. In 1939, while holidaying there, the writer Samuel Beckett heard the news of the outbreak of the Second World War in the La Touche Hotel. Another regular visitor to the area was the young John Millington Synge; on many occasions his mother moved the entire household to Greystones, where they rented a house for the summer. The actor Barry Fitzgerald also lived for a time in the town. During the 1970s the songwriter Jimmy Kennedy, most noted for 'South of the Border' and 'Red Sails in the Sunset', lived there for a number of years. A present resident of Greystones is the playwright Bernard Farrell, best known for his play *'I Do Not Love Thee, Dr Fell.'*

Greystones officially became a town only in 1984, when it elected its first Town Commissioners—now Greystones Town Council. The harbour is a popular area for sea sports, sailing, swimming, and shore angling competitions. There are two premier golf clubs in the vicinity, Greystones Golf Club and Charlesland. In recent years there has been extensive urban renewal to cater for the growing population, with a new sewerage scheme, shops, restaurants, and housing schemes extending from Blacklion to Charlesland. An interesting walk is the Cliff Walk, which runs parallel to the railway line to Bray. A recent addition to the town's amenities is the extension of the DART electric rail line from Bray in 2001.

KILCOOLE

The village of Kilcoole (*Cill Chomhghaill,* 'Comhghall's chapel') lies between Greystones and Newcastle and runs parallel to the sea. In 1021 the Hiberno-Norse of Dublin attempted to reorganise themselves in north Wicklow, but under their king, Sitric Mac Amhlaíbh, they were routed at Three Trouts, north of Kilcoole, by Giolla Chomhghaill Ó Tuathail. The O'Toole kingdom soon covered most of north Wicklow, from Kilcoole to Bray. It is recorded that in 1170 some Anglo-Norman soldiers attended Mass in Kilcoole church.

About the middle of the seventeenth century the O'Tooles were involved in a brief and bloody battle at Kilcoole. Sir Charles Coote was returning with his soldiers from an expedition at Wicklow, where they had recaptured the Black Castle, when they were attacked by a force led by the O'Tooles. The battle lasted about an hour; the insurgents lost twenty-seven men, including their leader, and had to withdraw.

In 1798 Kilcoole was a stronghold of the United Irishmen. Some of their members hid a keg of gunpowder in a mill on the Sea Road. The owner of the mill, John Kennedy, was a corporal in the Yeomanry but also a member of the United Irishmen. After taking delivery of the gunpowder from a man named James Toner, Kennedy reported it to the authorities. Toner was hanged, and his grave is in the overgrown graveyard. On another occasion Kennedy reported Thomas Maguire making his escape by boat. Maguire was arrested and was also hanged. Kennedy became an outcast and was despised in the area. In 1814, when he collapsed and died on the road, he was spat upon by passers-by. He was buried in the churchyard in Lotts Lane, and it is said that no vegetation has ever grown on his grave.

At 3 a.m. on 1 August 1914 three hundred members of the Irish Volunteers were mobilised to unload rifles and boxes of ammunition on the beach at Kilcoole from the *Kelpie*. Two RIC constables saw the vessel anchored off shore and became suspicious, but they were apprehended by armed men and held in the railway station. A motorboat and skiffs were used to bring the arms ashore, where they were transferred by lorry, car, and motorbike to Enniskerry and Dublin. In Kilcoole local Volunteers lined up four deep, shouldered their rifles, and marched up the Main Street singing 'A Nation Once Again'. In recent decades there has been speculation that shipments of arms were offloaded at isolated stretches of beach between Kilcoole and Arklow.

In 1982 Kilcoole became familiar to television viewers when RTE began filming the popular television serial 'Glenroe', with Joe Lynch (Dinny), Mick Lally (Miley), and Mary McEvoy (Biddy). Glenroe Farm became a favourite place for families to visit. The series was discontinued in 2001.

KILTEGAN

The neat village of Kiltegan (*Cill Téagáin*, 'Téagán's chapel') lies between Baltinglass and Hacketstown. Little is known about Téagán, but it is said that he was a member of the family of Uí Geintigh in Ossory and a follower of St Patrick. In 598 Kilranelagh, three miles from the village, was named as the site of the Battle of Dún Bolg, in which several kings were killed, and they are buried in the cemetery there.

By 1837 Kiltegan was a village of twenty-four houses and a dispensary. It also had a station of the Peace Preservation Force, an early police force established in 1816. Humewood Castle, one of the finest buildings in the county and described as the jewel in the crown of the architect William White, was built between 1867 and 1870 for the Hume family in Victorian gothic style, with the main rooms over a high basement, a security precaution taken in Fenian times.

Two miles from Kiltegan is High Park House, the home of generations of county squires, many of whom served as sheriff for Co. Wicklow. At the end of the seventeenth century the house and its estate of 508 acres (206 hectares) came into the possession of the Westby family. One of the family, Nicholas Westby, represented the area in the Irish Parliament and voted against the Act of Union. The house was burned during the 1798 Rising, and on the death of Nicholas Westby his brother Edward inherited the property and rebuilt the house. They were generous landlords and employed two hundred people to run the estate. Later John Hughes, a tea importer from Co. Down, bought the estate. In 1930 he made it available to St Patrick's Missionary Society.

Kiltegan was to produce one of the best handballers in Ireland in John Lawlor from Killalesh. Handball was unorganised in Lawlor's time, but games were played for a purse that could be as much as 400 sovereigns. In 1922 he became the first president of the Amateur Handball Association when the GAA took over administration of the game.

RATHDRUM

Before the Anglo-Norman invasion, Rathdrum (*Ráth Droma*, 'ring-fort of the ridge') was the fortress of the chieftains of the district then known as Críoch Chualann. In the late sixteenth century Fiach MacHugh O'Byrne and the O'Byrnes held the town. In 1595 the Lord Deputy, Sir William Fitzwilliam, an ancestor of Earl Fitzwilliam of Coolattin, captured it from them. In 1599 Rathdrum was the scene of a battle when the O'Tooles and the O'Byrnes slaughtered Sir Henry Harrington's forces. English officers were quoted as saying that some of their soldiers ran away from the battle; they were later captured and court-martialled. Harrington had come from England especially to put down the Wicklow septs, but the plan disintegrated and he was recalled.

In the eighteenth century the manufacture of flannel was the town's main industry. In 1793 a flannel hall was erected, an imposing building in the centre of the town. Rathdrum provided the market for those cottage industries, and the flannel hall became a large employer. At that time there were more than a thousand looms and spinning wheels in Co. Wicklow.

In May 1798 many of the workers at the Avoca mines left to join the rising. A director of the mines called Mills returned to the valley with a detachment of the Rathdrum Cavalry, where he collected all the available timber and took it in carts to fortify the flannel hall as barracks for the troops. In 1801, when the Act of Union came into force, cheaper flannel imports from Scotland and England meant that the industry declined and finally collapsed. On 16 November 1890 the flannel hall was accidentally burned down.

About the year 1806 a flour mill owned by the Tomlinson family began production and employed many of the redundant workers. In 1878 the mill was taken over by the Comerford family, and it continued in business until the twentieth century. A quarry also operated at nearby Balleece.

In 1798 a magistrate and commander of the Rathdrum Yeomanry, Captain Thomas King, lived at Kingston, near Rathdrum. He was a bloodthirsty man who resolved to bring Michael Dwyer to justice. He served on all the court-martials in the area and was responsible for many executions.

In 1841 a workhouse was opened in Rathdrum under the Poor Law to accommodate the growing numbers of rural poor. Destitute people had to apply for permission to enter the workhouse, where men and women (including married couples) lived in separate wings. There was an adjoining paupers' grave and an orphanage, which had a high mortality rate.

One of the most famous characters in the Rathdrum area was Thomas 'Buck' Whaley of Whaley Abbey, a man who won and lost a fortune. He engaged in some unusual gambles, including a wager that he would walk to Jerusalem and play handball against the walls of the Old City;

he did, and earned himself the additional nickname Jerusalem Whaley. The painter Cecil King was born in Rathdrum in 1921; he was a founder-member of the Contemporary Irish Art Society and of Rosc.

In 1995 Rathdrum was the location for a large crowd scene for the film *Michael Collins*, directed by Neil Jordan, when five thousand extras gathered in the town square for a dramatic sequence. In 1998 a cattle stampede through Rathdrum was organised for a film based on John B. Keane's novel *Durango*.

Today Rathdrum is the gateway to many of the county's beauty spots. The town is also known for its Synge and Parnell Summer Schools.

ROUNDWOOD

The village of Roundwood (*An Tóchar*, 'the causeway'), reputed to be the highest village in Ireland, dates from 1250. The causeway would have been a wooden structure that enabled travellers to pass over wet or marshy ground.

In the middle of the nineteenth century Dublin Corporation expressed concern about the quality and quantity of drinking-water in the city. A visiting specialist, Sir John Hawkshaw, suggested that they consider the Vartry River at Roundwood for a new, cleaner supply. There followed a prolonged period of disputes about rights and compensation for local landowners. Finally the obstacles were overcome and the scheme became a reality, and a reservoir was constructed in the bed of the Vartry. The main feature of the 400-acre (160-hectare) Vartry Waterworks is a great embankment, 1,600 feet (500 metres) long, 400 feet (120 metres) wide at the base and 30 feet (9 metres) wide at the top. It was estimated to hold two hundred days' supply for Dublin and the suburbs, at a daily rate of 12 million gallons. Entering projecting lips in a conspicuous water tower, the water runs into pipes and passes beneath the embankment, over filter beds and through a tunnel about two-and-a-half miles in length to a receiving-tank at Callagh Hill. From there the water passes through pipes laid mainly beneath the public roads and into reservoirs in Stillorgan, Co. Dublin. The new supply was inaugurated on 30 June 1863.

In 1939 a Fianna Fáil minister, Seán T. O'Kelly, came to live in Roundwood, and he was living there when he defeated Seán Mac Eoin in the election of 1945 to become the second President of Ireland. In 1959 he retired as President and returned to Roundwood. He died on 23 November 1966 at the age of eighty-four.

Derrylossary, about a mile south of the village, is known for its ruined church, which dates from the thirteenth century. The fourth President of Ireland, Erskine Childers, spent periods holidaying in nearby Glendalough House, and when he died suddenly on 17 November 1974 he was buried in the adjoining cemetery.

One of the best-known characters from Roundwood was William J. Duffy, postman, poet, and staunch GAA man. From 1901 to 1910 he was secretary of Co. Wicklow GAA. He joined the British army and for four years fought in France and Flanders in the Great War, winning a medal for bravery. He returned to Roundwood to become a postman, a local newspaper correspondent, and a prolific writer of ballads.

One of the proudest possessions of Roundwood was the St Laurence O'Toole Brass and Reed Band. It was formed in 1840 by Father John Gowan and played at parades and football matches and before such figures as Charles Stewart Parnell, Daniel O'Connell, and Father Theobald Mathew. It was disbanded in the 1950s. Thanks to the patronage of Erskine Childers senior, the village also had a pipe band. As well as helping with the organisation of the band, Childers also supplied the instruments.

WICKLOW

Wicklow (*Cill Mhantáin*, 'Mantán's chapel'), the county town, is half way along the county's coast, at the mouth of the Vartry River, where it is known as the Leitrim. The second-century Alexandrian astronomer Ptolemy (Claudius Ptolemaeus) mentions a place called Manapia in the vicinity of the present town of Wicklow.

The fifth-century bishop Palladius—precursor of Patrick—is said to have landed here and to have set up three churches before returning to Britain. According to legend, Patrick later landed in Wicklow close to the Black Castle.

In the eighth century the Vikings established a settlement at the estuary of the Vartry, naming it *Uíkar-ló* ('meadow of the bay'). In 1172 Wicklow was granted to Maurice Fitzgerald, ancestor of the Earls of

Meath. In 1178 he built the Black Castle, which was to be attacked many times by the O'Byrnes and the O'Tooles.

The town was granted a charter by King James I of England and another by King James II, and it was placed under a portreeve and burgesses. In 1214, when the monastery of Glendalough was destroyed, the O'Byrnes and O'Tooles, seeing the need for a replacement, founded a monastery for the conventual Franciscans in Wicklow. The fact that it came under the patronage of the O'Tooles explains its preservation during centuries of war and destruction. After the dissolution of the monasteries it was used as a courthouse and later as a store for war equipment.

In 1533 the O'Byrnes submitted to King Henry VIII and granted him the town and the castle. In 1580 the O'Tooles and Fiach MacHugh O'Byrne retook the castle. In 1641 Sir Charles Coote and his soldiers set fire to a small church in the town in which local people had sought refuge, and they were burned alive; thereafter the area was known as Melancholy Lane. In 1646 Colonel Luke O'Toole of Castlekevin recaptured the castle, but Oliver Cromwell routed him three years later.

In 1606 the area was created a county, and in 1613 Wicklow became its capital. The town returned three members to Parliament, more by virtue of ownership than by voting strength. Under King George IV, town commissioners were appointed; under the local government reform of 1898 these became Wicklow Urban District Council and in 2001 Wicklow Town Council.

In 1761 construction of the harbour began. Additional piers were built over the years, the East Pier in 1880 and the Packet Pier five years later. Before the First World War up to sixty ships operated from the harbour, which gave employment to more than two hundred dockers. The Hamilton, Dolittle, Pim, Darragh, Flanagan, and Edwards families were some of the well-known shipowners.

One of the blackest spots in Wicklow was the county gaol at Kilmantan Hill, erected in 1702 principally to house prisoners under the Penal Laws. In 1798 crowds attended the public hanging of insurgents. During this period the lives of priests were constantly in danger. In 1799 the parish priest, Father Andrew O'Toole, was returning to his home when three men attacked and killed him. An old woman gathering sticks witnessed the murder, but she soon disappeared and was never seen again. The culprits were never apprehended.

In 1820 nine men set out walking from Wicklow to Dublin. Short of funds, they stole from neighbouring clotheslines. They were apprehended and hanged.

Wicklow is a favourite tourist centre, and in summer large numbers are attracted to the sandy beaches at nearby Brittas Bay and Silver Strand. Brittas, with three miles of golden sand, is one of the most popular resorts on the east coast. The sand-dunes sheltering the beach have many species of wildlife and plants. One of the highlights of the year is the Wicklow Regatta. Wicklow Gaol is now open to the public as a museum.

9 COMMUNICATIONS *and* TRAVEL

IN 1789 *The* MAIL coach went into operation to serve the principal towns, making communication and travel considerably easier. In 1790 the enterprising Tobias Toole established a mail-coach service between Dublin and Bray. In west Wicklow the mail cars stopped at the Downshire Hotel en route to Waterford and Kilkenny; while the horses were being changed, the passengers enjoyed refreshments in the hotel. The mail coach followed the road by Woodenbridge and Arklow. Horses for the service were also changed and stabled in Redcross.

In 1811 a new mail-coach route was inaugurated, linking Dublin with Wicklow and Wexford, passing through Bray, the one point at which the River Dargle was then bridged. The road southwards then went via Windgates to Delgany, on through Kilcoole to Ashford and a stop at Hunter's Hotel. A decision was taken to open a more direct route through Kilmacanogue and the Glen of the Downs. In 1814 the route was completed and a new coach, the Waterloo, travelling to Waterford, was introduced on the new road. The journey from Dublin to Wicklow took five-and-a-half hours, with coaches setting out at 6 a.m., stopping for breakfast at Bray, and arriving in Wicklow about 11:30 a.m. The fare from Dublin to Bray was 3s 9d for a passenger travelling inside and 2*s* *6d* for travelling outside with the luggage.

At that time there were many complaints about the deplorable state of the roads in the county. Steps were taken to raise revenue for their repair by erecting turnpikes (toll gates) on the roads leading into Bray and other large towns. With the mail coaches passing through Bray, it was decided to erect a turnpike at Violet Hill. Only then did the people of the town express their opposition to the road system and turnpike charges, and there were many protest meetings.

From 1816 the Italian businessman Charles Bianconi began running jaunting-cars and coaches on a number of routes. By the mid-1820s he was operating a more regular coach service from Dublin to Wexford, stopping at Kilcoole for refreshments. Enniskerry, with its close proximity to the Powerscourt Estate, became a post town, and a mail and stage-coach service, together with jaunting-cars, commuted daily between there and Dublin. In Bray, Quin's Hotel was another popular stopping-off point for coaches travelling between Dublin and Wicklow. By 1832, when the turnpikes committee made its report, local people decided that rather than cause further disruption they would suffer the inconvenience and expense of the system.

WILLIAM DARGAN AND *The* RAILWAY

In 1833 the first railway in Ireland was completed between Dublin and Kingstown (Dún Laoghaire). From this time onwards there were numerous proposals for railways, particularly from Dublin southwards towards Rosslare and Waterford. Various groups fought for control of the scheme, and an engineer, William Dargan, had to mediate and streamline the process. Dargan, born in Carlow in 1799, had trained as an engineer and surveyor with Thomas Telford and had worked on the Holyhead project.

In 1845 a new company was formed to obtain the necessary parliamentary powers to build a line from Dublin to Wicklow, Wexford, and Waterford. This company, the Dublin and Wicklow Railway Company, acquired control of the Dublin–Kingstown line. When Dargan became involved in extending the railway to Bray, the project was mired in economic problems. He reorganised it as an autonomous Irish concern, with himself as a director and later chairman.

The construction of the Bray line, which employed three hundred labourers, began in August 1847. On 8 July 1854 the first train from

Dublin arrived in Bray Station, carrying the directors of the company. Simultaneously another company, the Dublin, Dundrum, and Rathfarnham Railway, constructed a separate inland route from Dublin to Bray, forming a junction with the Dalkey–Bray route at Shanganagh, Co. Dublin, just north of Bray. This line ran via Dundrum to Harcourt Street Station in Dublin.

If the railway provided the conditions for the growth of Bray, it was Dargan's foresight that made the prospect a reality. He was not the first businessman to realise the potential, nor the first to develop it, but he was the one who contributed most to the emerging resort. He set out to mould Bray into a fashionable area, using Brighton as a model. His first independent project in the town was to take a long lease from the Earl of Meath on the ground running parallel to the shore. He cleared the area, converting it into a grassy promenade and esplanade. Opposite the beach he constructed many fine terraces of excellent houses. Next he built the Turkish baths, in a Middle Eastern style. Dargan was at the height of his prestige with the success of his railway projects and his ambitious Great Dublin Industrial Exhibition. Queen Victoria was so impressed when she visited the exhibition that she offered him a baronetcy, but he declined the offer.

With the completion of the railway to Bray, construction work in the town accelerated. Prominent Dublin businessmen built elegant houses and villas along the seashore and adjoining roads. The railway gave Bray access not only to Dublin but also to the port of Kingstown and its links to Britain. In the two decades from 1851 the population of the town rose from 4,151 to 6,500. Over the next twenty-five years Bray was to receive a gas works, public lighting, and a new harbour.

Following the success of the line to Bray, the directors planned to continue the railway to Wicklow. It was also planned to extend it to Rosslare, where a cross-channel service would link the port to Fishguard. The Earl of Meath would not permit the line to run through his estate at Kilruddery, but he gave the company the Bray Head route instead, running parallel to the shore, free of charge. The construction of the Bray–Wicklow section began under Dargan's directorship, with Isambard Kingdom Brunel as chief engineer.

Brunel had won fame as an engineer from his work on the huge steamship *Great Eastern* and his impressive bridges. His expertise proved invaluable in the construction of the railway. The first 5 miles (8 kilometres) along the cliffs involved three tunnels and four wooden trestle bridges; this section of line became known as Brunel's Folly, on which many contractors and up to five hundred workers were employed. The Bray Head problems delayed the opening of the Dublin–Wicklow line until 13 October 1855.

In August 1867 a serious accident occurred when the Enniscorthy–Dublin train left the track at the side of Bray Head and fell 30 feet (9 metres). Two passengers were killed, and twenty-three others were injured.

Lord Meath was a benevolent landlord. Besides donating land for the railway he undertook many capital works at his own expense, including the building of the town hall and market place. The esteem in which he was held is evident from the many eminent guests who were entertained in Kilruddery, many of whom travelled to Bray by train and were transferred to Kilruddery by coach. Among his guests were King George IV, the Prince and Princess of Wales, several Lord Mayors of London, and William Gladstone.

Until the coming of the railway to Greystones in 1855 the town had consisted of ten houses and a small pier, but the new link with Dublin was to see rapid development in the area. The advent of the railway marked a new beginning for Bray, Greystones, Wicklow, and Arklow. The service was advertised as suitable for holidays by the sea and for people travelling to business in the city. Kilcoole was also to reap the benefit of the new railway line, and a station was built on the sea side of the tracks. Drovers brought herds of cattle and flocks of sheep from the surrounding areas to the marshalling yards at Kilcoole Station for transporting to Dublin. Over the years the line at Kilcoole suffered from coastal erosion.

The Railway Act (1864) authorised a branch line to diverge from the main line to allow trains to operate to and from Arklow and Woodenbridge meeting at the Junction Station. At Woodenbridge there were two platforms for main-line trains and one for the branch line. On leaving Woodenbridge the line crossed the Aughrim River by an iron bridge before climbing to Aughrim. It was a busy line and brought many tourists to explore the vicinity. At Arklow the railway connected with the older mine tramway, which was used to draw ore from the Avoca mines to Arklow harbour.

In 1906 legislation changed the title of the railway to the Dublin and South-Eastern Railway Company. By the early twentieth century five trains were running each way daily. The service to Woodenbridge closed in 1964.

SHIPPING

The area from Wicklow Head to Dublin Bay was one of the most treacherous stretches along the east coast, making travel by sea extremely hazardous. In an effort to alleviate this danger the engineer John Trail was commissioned to design a unique pair of octagonal lighthouses, known as the Upper and Lower Towers; and on 1 September 1781 the lighthouse on Wicklow Head went into service. Two towers were necessary to distinguish them from Hook Head for ships approaching from the east. The lanterns of the 95-foot (29-metre) cut-stone towers were approximately 250 feet (75 metres) above sea level and were visible for more than 20 miles (30 kilometres).

Despite the aid of lighthouses, many ships sailing to Dublin from the south were blown off course onto the rocky headlands off Wicklow Head and Bray Head. Many of their cargoes were washed up on beaches, where local people often plundered them. One such shipwreck occurred on Christmas Day 1784 when the *Friendship* was washed up at Bray and local people enjoyed the booty of wine and fruit. In 1818 oil lamps replaced the original mirrors and six candles on the Wicklow Head lighthouses.

The isolated and rugged coastline of Co. Wicklow proved suitable for another lucrative trade: smuggling. The smugglers would carry out their illegal trade under cover of darkness or in misty conditions to avoid detection by the 'preventive men'. Corruption was rife among Revenue and Customs officers, who frequently accepted bribes, and the authorities failed to curb the practice. The smugglers would anchor off shore and transfer their contraband tea, brandy, silk, or other commodities to smaller boats and take them ashore at concealed coves and caves. Some of the favourite landing-places were Kilcoole, Wicklow Head, and Clogga Strand at Arklow. From the aptly named Brandy Hole on the eastern slope of Bray Head contraband was hauled up with a rope and pulley and hidden in caves and the ancient Ráithín a Chluig ('little fort of the bell') church. From there it was transferred by road to inns and merchants as far away as Dublin.

The first lifeboat service to be established in Ireland by the Royal National Lifeboat Institute was in Arklow. In December 1824 the Inspector-General of Coastguards in Dublin asked for a lifeboat service to be established at Arklow. This was imperative, as there had been four serious shipwrecks in the area in the previous three years. A 24-foot

(7-metre) eight-oared boat was commissioned. The Arklow Bank, 6 miles (10 kilometres) east of Arklow and 13 miles (21 kilometres) long, was one of the most dangerous obstacles in the Irish Sea, having been responsible for many shipwrecks over several decades. In 1825 a lightship, the *Star,* was positioned at the bank to warn oncoming ships of the danger.

In 1834 a coastguard station was established in Bray, close to the martello tower. The main functions of the station were to be on the alert for smuggling, to watch out for wrecks, to rescue people in difficulties, and to be vigilant for a possible French invasion. The members of the service were recruited from among former seamen.

In 1843 there was a series of shipwrecks off Wicklow Head, including that of the *Peggy and Jane,* carrying coal to Dublin. In February 1848, during a fierce storm, the *Calypso* was driven ashore, but the Arklow lifeboat was fortunate in being able to rescue all eighteen men on board. The following year the *Wanderer* was wrecked off Greystones. In 1852 a cargo ship, the *Lady Harriet,* was wrecked off Bray. In 1856 a gale led to the collision and sinking of two collier-brigs off Bray Head. In 1865 five ships went down off the Co. Wicklow coast, including the *Tonquin,* in which all eleven members of the crew were drowned. In 1863, in an effort to reduce the alarming number of shipwrecks, a light-vessel, the *Wicklow Swash,* was moored off Arklow.

From the middle of the nineteenth century the commercial life of Co. Wicklow's coastal towns flourished. Harbour improvements at Wicklow allowed larger vessels with deeper draughts to enter the port. These included a breakwater and the Steam Packet Pier and East Pier, with new access roads. There was substantial growth in the export of timber, livestock, particularly sheep, and general cargoes, giving employment to more than two hundred dockers. Arklow was also a busy port, with an import and export trade and more than eighty vessels, making it the largest schooner port in Ireland at the time. Exports from the Avoca Mines were a lucrative source of income, while the port's merchant fleet carried cargo from as far away as the Mediterranean. A large fishing fleet was also based in the port. For a time the Arklow fleet operated a barter system, with oysters being exchanged for coal from England.

The harbour at Bray was under construction for many years before it was completed in 1897. Hitherto vessels found difficulty in navigating the mouth of the river because of heavy silting. Cargoes had to be transferred from ships to smaller boats, called flats, at low tide and landed on the beach. The harbour provided a profitable business, as Welsh colliers delivered coal weekly to Bray merchants and the local gasworks. Slate was also imported, while timber and grain were exported.

10 VISITORS To CO. WICKLOW in The NINETEENTH CENTURY

'WHEREVER WE moved in the course of our Wicklow tour, we were equally surprised to find such excellent roads, and no turnpikes. The cabins, which lay in our route, were also neat, generally whitewashed, and an air of comfort and plenty breathed throughout; before each door were the finest pigs and poultry. The peasant and his wife were tolerably well dressed; and their children, of which each cabin has a bountiful quota, looked fat, fresh, and ruddy. Here, as in every part of Ireland, which I visited, a dog was almost always one of the inmates of every cabin.' –John Carr, *Stranger in Ireland* (1806).

'Down the hill to Powerscourt, a grand domain, with very grand trees. The Dargle, superior even to its fame–an indiscriminately beautiful mixture of wood, water, rocks, hill, valley . . . Drove by Dunran to the Devil's Glen, which is a glen with wooded crags and a stream brawling below, not unlike many in Scotland, though, I think, rather on a more extensive scale than any I can remember there. Passed through the grounds of several gentlemen, and, of course, saw the exterior of many charming places. Kilruddery, Lord Meath's seat, a new Gothic chateau, surrounded with very fine antique gardens, the scene of "the Irish Hunt." Rosanna, the scene of Miss Edgeworth's tale, a singularly beautiful lane with oak boughs reaching clear over it. Luncheon at Newrath, and dinner (late) at Old Connaught, near Bray, the seat of the Attorney-General Plunkett.'–*Sir Walter Scott's Tour in Ireland in 1825.*

'The scenery of Wicklow is petite; and I can only explain what I mean to the travelled reader, by saying that it resembles in this character the "Mountains of the Rhine." The hills, or rocks, or eminence, which borders that "abounding and exulting river", are mountains to the imagination. They possess the form without the bulk, the majesty without the height, of the colossi of nature. Their grandeur does not arise from the massiveness, but from shape and combination of beauty that we easily suppose the effect to be assisted in some measure by an intermingling of the sublime.'–Leitch Ritchie, *Ireland Picturesque and Romantic* (1837–38).

'A two-horse car, which will accommodate twelve, or will condescend to receive twenty passengers, starts from the railway station for Bray, running along the coast for the chief part of the journey, though you have but few views of the sea, on account of intervening woods and hills. The whole of this country is covered with handsome villas and their gardens, and pleasure grounds. There are round many of the houses parks of some extent, and always of considerable beauty, among the trees of which the road winds.

'After leaving Bray, with its pleasant bay, and pleasant river, and pleasant inn, the little Wicklow tour may be said to commence properly; and, as that romantic and beautiful country has been described many times in familiar terms, our only chance is to speak thereof in romantic and beautiful language, such as no other writer can possibly have employed.'–W. M. Thackeray, *The Irish Sketch-Book* (1842).

'So wonderful and remarkable a scene I had really never before seen. Wild, bare, rocky, and dark-coloured mountain ran out in a sharp promontory; to the right the ground descends into the valley of Glendassan, and to the left that of Glendalough. One can see into both these valleys at the same time, through broad, wide rock-doors. In the foreground, in the midst of the basin formed by the meeting of the two valleys, lies the low ruins of the Seven Churches; and right to the centre, forming the middle point of the landscape, rises the lofty, slender, pillar-temple, that stands, in good preservation, exactly in the middle of this picturesque wilderness, like Pompeii's Pillar in the midst of the waste of Alexandria.' J. G. Kohl, *Travels in Ireland* (1844).

'Nearing the northern opening of the glen, about four miles from Bray, a flat velvet sward, reached by a rustic gateway and bridge, leads to a romantic cottage. Behind this, up the umbrageous bank, runs a pathway leading to the Octagon Temple, which, situated on the very crown of the bank, commands one of the noblest prospects in the county of Wicklow. Far below lie the dark masses of the glen, and right opposite rises the lofty Sugar loaf, the road winding like a white ribbon through the valley between it and its lesser namesake. The glen is about half a mile long, its sides being clothed with verdure and presenting an agreeable retreat from the glare of the summer sun. It is supposed to have been in remote ages the bed of a mountain torrent, the waters of which have long since been diverted into another channel by the volcanic action which has brought about many important changes in the earth's surface.'—*Carson's Illustrated Guide of the County of Wicklow* (1882).

11 MODERN TIMES

JOHN REDMOND

The **BRITISH PRIME MINISTER**, H. H. Asquith, needed Irish support to secure the passing of the Parliament Bill (1911), and he approached the leading member of the Irish Party, John Redmond, for his support. Redmond agreed, in return for support for the Home Rule Bill, which became law in September 1914 but was suspended for the duration of the First World War (1914–18), which had just begun.

At first Redmond ignored the Irish Volunteers, but he was to reverse this decision. On 20 September 1914, when Redmond stopped at Woodenbridge, Co. Wicklow, on his way home to Aughavanagh, he addressed the Irish Volunteers on parade in a field adjoining the station. He pledged support for England in the war for the 'defence of small nations.' He called on Irishmen to join the British army, 'wherever the firing line extends, in defence of right, of freedom, and of religion in this war.' The speech was to cause a split between the Irish Republican Brotherhood and those who supported Redmond's call. Redmond sought the support of Lord Meath and his endorsement for the Volunteers, but this was not forthcoming.

Militant nationalists reacted angrily, but the great majority of the Volunteers answered his call. Redmond's followers became known as the National Volunteers. Almost 200,000 Irishmen joined the British army, although in 1918 there was an anti-conscription riot in Wicklow.

The 1918 ELECTION

In 1838 Thomas Barton bought Glendalough House in Annamoe. He was a benevolent landlord who financed the reroofing of all the small houses in the village. His son, Robert Barton, was to become one of the leading figures in the first Dáil Éireann. In the 1918 general election the Wicklow-Kildare constituency returned Barton and J. R. Etchingham, the latter then in jail. Following their victory in the election, supporters of the Irish Volunteers decided to establish an independent Irish parliament. Other Irish MPs were invited to join them and to abstain from the British Parliament.

Only twenty-seven members were available to attend the first session of Dáil Éireann in the Mansion House, Dublin, on 21 January 1919, as many were in jail. By the second session, on 1 April, the British Prime Minister, David Lloyd George, had ordered the release of the internees. At the Dáil session Éamon de Valera was elected President, and Robert Barton was appointed Minister for Agriculture. Barton was arrested and sentenced to imprisonment in Mountjoy Jail but escaped later that year. He left a note for the governor, stating that he could not stay any longer as he was unhappy with the service.

In the next general election, on 19 May 1920, Barton was returned for Co. Wicklow, together with Art O'Connor, Domhnall Ó Buachalla, Erskine Childers, and Christopher Byrne. Barton was one of the Irish delegation, with Michael Collins and Arthur Griffith, at the Anglo-Irish Treaty negotiations in London on 11 October 1921. For the third Dáil election, on 16 June 1922, de Valera and Collins made a pact in which all candidates would stand as Sinn Féin and would form a joint government. The five candidates elected for Co. Wicklow were Robert Barton, Christopher Byrne, James Everett, Richard Wilson, and Hugh Colohan. The same year Barton was interned, but he was released the following year and returned to his farm at Annamoe.

The WAR OF INDEPENDENCE

In May 1914 there was celebration throughout the county on the passing of the Home Rule Bill. Torchlight processions were organised, with bands and political speeches.

In the opening minutes of the Great War the Germans captured two Arklow ships' masters in Hamburg; eight other Arklow men serving on other ships were also arrested that day. They were unfortunate to be in German ports as war was declared, and they were interned in the stables of Ruhleben racecourse in the Berlin suburb of Spandau and were not released until October 1918. Many Wicklow men had enlisted in the British army, and the county council established a county distress committee to assist the dependants of those killed.

Co. Wicklow was to escape the worst of the conflict from the 1916 Rising to the Civil War (1917–23). Big houses were burned down and looted, and there were arson attacks on military installations. The Carysfort mansion, Shelton Abbey, was one of the first houses burned, and many RIC barracks in the county were also attacked.

In 1916, with the outbreak of hostilities, there was heightened security around the Kynoch explosives factory in Arklow. The 3rd Battalion of the Leinster Regiment patrolled the perimeter of the factory, while the Royal Artillery mounted guns for seaward defences. The North Beach was declared out of bounds. Despite the extra protection, on 5 February 1920 the IRA carried out a raid to capture gelignite and TNT. They had received information that Kynoch was shipping gelignite to Birmingham. When the ship was loaded with its cargo they commandeered a yawl in the harbour and boarded it, took the $2\frac{1}{2}$ tons of explosives, and buried it on the beach until it was required for operations. In a second raid, on 13 November 1920, the IRA successfully captured a large quantity of explosives and transported it to Dublin.

The Dublin–Wexford railway line was one of the most sabotaged lines in the country. The IRA constantly damaged the track and planted bombs. The service was sparse south of Bray because of fear of attack. One locomotive was steel-plated and used for hauling an armoured train. In the winter of 1920 the entire county was placed under curfew: anyone found out of doors after 10 p.m. without a pass was liable to be arrested, or shot; but people found ways around these restrictions.

A man standing by his door near the town hall in Bray was shot dead by the Black and Tans. In 1921 the IRA unit in Bray launched an attack on the Black and Tans and RIC manning the courthouse and barracks. Fire was returned, and battle raged for two hours. Later that night there followed widespread arrests of suspected IRA members in the locality. The old Wicklow Gaol became the headquarters of the Cheshire

Regiment and a prison for revolutionaries. In 1922–24 the Free State army occupied the jail.

On 7 January 1922 a vote in Dáil Éireann resulted in a majority (64 to 57) in favour of accepting the Anglo-Irish Treaty. Éamon de Valera led those who rejected the Treaty. In Co. Wicklow the political divisions created widespread disruption and destruction. The railway line and many bridges were blown up; roads were damaged and blocked to prevent the transfer of supplies and men. Rate collectors were often held up as a source of funds. Both sides engaged in guerrilla tactics. The Irregulars attacked a garrison at the Royal Hotel, Glendalough, and the Baltinglass Workhouse was attacked and burned. The fever hospital in Shillelagh was occupied by the military.

The most important engagement in Co. Wicklow took place in Blessington in July 1922. As fighting continued in Dublin, anti-Treaty reinforcements had been ordered to muster in Blessington before marching on the capital. A column of more than a hundred men from south Tipperary led by Mick Sheehan stationed itself there, having answered Oscar Traynor's request for forces to reinforce the republicans in Dublin. They took over buildings and commandeered transport and provisions. Traynor and Ernie O'Malley joined units from the South Dublin Brigade and Kildare. Morale among the members was low, and they launched some hit-and-run raids on surrounding villages, including Brittas and Ballymore Eustace. Meanwhile the forces of the Provisional Government moved southwards through the mountains towards Blessington, well equipped with armoured cars and infantry. After some exchanges of fire the anti-Treatyites retreated. More than sixty of them were arrested, and the attack on Dublin was aborted.

The death of the IRA chief of staff, Liam Lynch, in April 1923 ended republican resistance. The Civil War left a legacy of bitterness in communities and families that prevailed for many decades.

SOCIAL AND ECONOMIC CHANGE

1900–1920

The greatest problem besetting the county in the early years of the twentieth century was a chronic shortage of houses. One overdue improvement had been the demolition of poor cabins and the introduction of the Housing of the Working Classes (Ireland) Act (1896), under which new streets containing artisan dwellings were erected throughout the county. In 1900 Bray, with the largest population in the county, was first to receive local authority houses, in Dargan Street, Ardee Street, and Maitland Street in Little Bray. A sales system was begun, with loans provided by the Commissioners of Public Works. Under this scheme 155 houses were bought by artisans in Bray and 112 in Arklow, with loans being repaid over a period of thirty years.

Under the Labourers (Ireland) Act (1906) the district councils dramatically accelerated the building of labourers' cottages throughout the county, but a succession of wars at home and abroad, followed by the setting up of the new state, greatly curtailed house-building and the previous progressive trend.

On 1 January 1904 the Motor Car Act (1903) came into operation for the registration and licensing of cars and motorcycles by local authorities. By 8 January Michael Rahilly of Bray (later to be killed during the 1916 Rising) and Muriel Bland of Kilquade became the first man and first woman to be granted a licence in Co. Wicklow. There was a speed limit of 20 miles per hour for cars, but even this was considered excessive for Co. Wicklow's rural roads, which had hitherto to contend only with horse-drawn vehicles. A deterioration of the road surfaces was inevitable under the extra strain from motorised traffic. Wicklow County Council, conscious of extra maintenance costs, proposed a limit of 10 miles per hour through towns and villages. In 1908 an inquiry was held to decide on an appropriate speed limit. After much lobbying by vested interests a limit of 12 miles per hour was imposed on selected roads at Glendalough, Greystones, Rathnew, and Newtownmountkennedy.

Bray frequently suffered serious flooding from high tides and the overflowing of the Dargle River in Little Bray. Many of the houses were one-storey cottages, and the water often rose to roof level, doing untold damage to buildings and belongings. In August 1905 a fierce storm struck the east coast, and more than five inches of rain fell in the Bray area in a period of 36 hours. The Dargle burst its banks, and water rose to a height of 11 feet (over 3 metres), flooding the entire area. Approximately four hundred families, comprising more than two thousand people, were made homeless. But emergency services went into action, and the distressed people were taken from their homes in boats and given refuge in the town hall and various other buildings.

One man, James Plunkett, was drowned in the flood, and homes and property were damaged beyond repair. The Little Bray Relief Fund was established, and Lord Meath appealed for subscriptions to assist the beleaguered families. There was an overwhelming response, and clothing and bedding stores were opened throughout the town. But despite the spirit of good will there was looting from unoccupied houses by unscrupulous youths.

From the beginning of the twentieth century tuberculosis was endemic in Ireland, so much so that it was known as the 'Irish disease'. One in every nine death certificates recorded at that time gave TB as the cause of death. County councils and corporations were authorised to open clinics and sanatoriums in an effort to combat this plague. Newcastle Hospital in Co. Wicklow was the first purpose-built TB hospital in Ireland. Florence Wynne, of a well-known Co. Wicklow family, was the driving force behind the venture, obtaining a grant from Lord Fitzwilliam of twenty acres and financial support. Another strong supporter of the hospital was the Marchioness of Aberdeen and Temair, wife of the Lord Lieutenant. In 1907 she founded the Women's National Health Association, which educated people on preventive medicine. She opened the Wicklow branch with a tuberculosis exhibition that she described as 'an exhibition of horrors'. Co. Wicklow was particularly badly hit by the disease, and the hospital was soon full to capacity. There were 223 deaths from TB in 1911 in Co. Wicklow, while a further 1,784 were suffering from the disease. Many families were ashamed of the stigma of TB and wrote to patients with the disease at Anchor Hotel, Newcastle. The postmen were aware of the true destination of the mail.

Industry in Co. Wicklow had been spasmodic and mainly confined to the coastal towns and the north of the county. Between 1895 and 1919 the Kynoch explosives and munitions factory in Arklow employed up to four thousand people. The outbreak of the Great War gave an enormous boost to output at the factory, followed immediately by a recruitment drive. Special trains transferred workers from as far as Co. Wexford to operate the plant; but the trains proved too expensive, and in 1916 the company built huts for workers from outside the area. The huts were in constant use, as the men were on shift work. On 21 September 1917 there was an explosion in the factory, in which twenty-seven people were killed and many more injured. The factory ceased production in 1919.

Bray, with its larger work force and its proximity to Dublin and its port, was to be the most industrialised of the Co. Wicklow towns. In the early part of the twentieth century the principal industries were Smithson's flour mills and the distillers Watkins, Jameson, and Pim. Several businesses supplied growing transport needs, including Thompson's Carriage Works and Sawmills, and Colliers, which later expanded into the undertaking business.

Wicklow did not attract the range of industry to be found in Bray and Arklow. The town's main industries were centred on the harbour and maritime activities. In 1910 the West Pier was constructed, and over the following years further improvements were undertaken around the harbour area.

The 1920s

In November 1920 Wicklow County Council brought to the attention of the Forestry Department of Dáil Éireann the wholesale felling of timber by 'enemy agents'. They asked that immediate action be taken to safeguard the forests of Glendalough, the Glen of the Downs, Powerscourt, and the Scalp. In June 1922 the county council passed a resolution calling on the government to promote a scheme of purchasing rugged land suitable for forestry. By the 1920s most of the workhouses had been closed, and outdoor relief (welfare payments to those not housed in workhouses) was administered more freely.

Until the 1920s only oil lamps lit many towns and villages in Co. Wicklow. From the mid-1920s the ESB began to connect many areas with electricity, including Avoca, Baltinglass, Blessington, Carnew, Dunlavin, Tinahely, Enniskerry, and Rathdrum, but it was some time before smaller communities were connected to the grid. From 1925 street lighting was introduced to many villages. In the quarter of a century to 1924, 731 rural cottages were built, from Rathdown to Killincarrig, Ballyknockan, and Carnew.

In 1924 a large artificial reservoir in the bed of the Vartry River was developed. Beside the reservoir new filter beds were laid out, through which the pipes would take the water to Dublin.

In 1929 the local authority estimated that 550 houses were needed in Bray and 202 in Wicklow, to cope with the growing population.

The 1930s

Unemployment rose sharply following the Wall Street crash of October 1929 and the economic depression that reached Ireland the following year. The general election of 1932 brought Fianna Fáil to power, and the new government introduced a number of social policies to relieve distress. One measure was the Housing (Financial and Miscellaneous Provisions) Act (1932), under which the government contributed between a third and two-thirds of the cost of local housing. Despite having elected only one Fianna Fáil deputy, Co. Wicklow was to benefit reasonably well from the scheme. In 1934 cottages were built in the smaller villages of Rathnew and Ballygannon, Rathdrum. Under this initiative, known as the 'village scheme', 188 houses were also built in Baltinglass, Blessington, Dunlavin, Newtownmountkennedy, Kilcoole, Aughrim, Tinahely, Greystones, and Rathnew.

Bray Urban District Council declared many houses in the Little Bray area unfit for human habitation. These were demolished, and the inhabitants were rehoused in a new scheme of 268 houses in Wolfe Tone Square. Smaller local authority housing schemes were also developed in St Cronan's Road and Kilmantan Park. By 1939 Wicklow Board of Health had built 1,043 houses under the Housing Acts, the largest number built by any local authority. Despite the lack of finance and facilities, the lives of many people were improved. Private housing was also on the increase, and many bungalows distinctive of east coast resorts were built in Bray and Greystones.

By the mid-1930s industry began to recover, and the opening of Arklow Pottery in 1934 was to be a boost to local employment. Many potters came from the ceramic industry in Stoke-on-Trent, and workers were recruited from the surrounding districts of Cos. Wicklow and Wexford. The company grew to be a large employer and developed a reputation for first-class products. Larger factories were also established during the 1930s, including those of W. and E. W. Haughton, manufactures of ink and gum, and Solus, manufacturers of light-bulbs, both in Bray. During this decade the commercial aspect of the harbour declined, but there was a growth in its development as a venue for pleasure craft.

In 1938 the inhabitants of the townland of Valleymount in north-west Co. Wicklow were informed that they would have to leave their homes to facilitate the ESB's damming of the River Liffey and King River and flooding the area to provide power for the hydro-electric station at

Poulaphouca, and to increase the water supply to Dublin. Local politicians and the people of Valleymount were opposed to the scheme, but their protests were in vain; by the end of 1938 they had accepted the inevitable, and evacuations had begun. Seventy-six houses and several bridges were demolished, lest they later prove an underwater hazard. An ancient holy well also had to be sacrificed. The old burial ground of Burgage was also inundated, but the ESB provided a new cemetery, and remains were exhumed and re-interred near Blessington. The 309 residents of Valleymount received compensation and were widely dispersed to Ballyknockan, Hollywood, Kildare, and Dublin. The Poulaphouca Reservoir flooded 6,500 acres (2,600 hectares). In the early 1940s there was a milk shortage in the surrounding villages of Lacken and Ballyknockan, due to the lack of cows.

The 1940s

From the outbreak of the Second World War in 1939, the flow of imported goods to Ireland began to dry up. Tea, bread, sugar, and clothing were in short supply, and rationing was introduced. Fuel for heat and power was particularly scarce. Turf became the main substitute for coal, and orders were issued for the harvesting of turf and the storing of supplies. Road maintenance and housing construction were greatly curtailed, and hundreds of construction workers were laid off.

At the beginning of 1940 the Government decided to raise a voluntary force, known as the Local Security Force, as a precaution against a possible German invasion, and throughout Co. Wicklow large numbers enrolled. In 1940 parish guilds were established throughout the county to help alleviate poverty. This was a system of voluntary committees to assist the work of the County Commissioners. In July 1940 a particularly energetic guild was established in Bray; it raised funds for the planting of six acres of potatoes and despatched a hundred unemployed men to Glencree Bog to cut turf for distribution to the poor of the parish.

Wicklow suffered indirectly from the effects of the war. With the danger to shipping in the Irish Sea, the town's lucrative import-export business was undermined, and the harbour was virtually empty of schooners and steamers. However, the Harbours Act (1947) established a new harbour authority in the town, which promoted extensive work, including the provision of a new berth on the North Quay and repairs to the Steam Packet Pier and East Pier.

During the war several merchant ships built in Arklow were lost in the Pacific and Atlantic Oceans. The town's Maritime Museum houses displays associated with these grim events.

In 1946 Co. Wicklow was still recording sixty-five deaths a year from TB. The development of the BCG vaccine in the 1930s was a breakthrough in the fight against the disease. When it became available, children were vaccinated, and other enlightened measures helped to alleviate the misery. The Housing (Amendment) Act (1946) allocated grants for the building of an extra room in the homes of infected people, allowing them to be treated in their own home while maintaining a degree of segregation and so helping to prevent the spread of the disease to other family members.

Co. Wicklow slowly adjusted to life after the war, but it was not until 1948 that the county council became actively involved again in new housing and road schemes.

The 1950s

In 1951 Wire Ropes began production on the north quays in Wicklow harbour. This was an exception, as other factories throughout the county were laying off workers. From 1952 the country was to suffer another economic depression, which resulted in a significant increase in emigration, then at an average of 40,000 a year. In 1956 the mining industry in Avoca received a boost when St Patrick's Mining Company, a subsidiary of a Canadian company, began operations. A number of new industries were established in Bray, including Beverley Bags and a glass bottle factory on the Boghall Road. The most significant industry was Industrial Yarns, whose textile factory at maximum capacity employed more than two hundred people. Other industries in Bray at this period included the sweet manufacturer Kennymore, Coughlan's toothpaste factory, and Coxon's wallpaper factory. In 1956 Bray Chamber of Commerce was established. In 1958 the opening of Ardmore Studios gave employment to craft workers in north Co. Wicklow. In the Boghall area of Bray several industrial estates were established, attracting a number of diverse industries.

The expected housing boom became a reality only in the late 1950s. Though the tourism importance of the town was on the wane, building workers were kept in constant employment, with an mixture of new private and local authority housing. The building of private houses in Bray and its environs was a notable feature of this period. Local authority housing schemes were constructed at Palermo, Fassaroe, and St Peter's Road.

By 1955 the death rate in Co. Wicklow from TB had dropped to 16 a year, and the last patients were transferred from Newcastle to Peamount Hospital in Newcastle, Co. Dublin. The Minister for Health in the first coalition Government (1948–51), Dr Noël Browne, launched a campaign to eradicate TB. He later lived and practised as a GP in Bray for a number of years.

The 1960s

The election of Seán Lemass as Taoiseach in 1959 was to see a change in the country, heralding a period of unprecedented industrial growth and prosperity. Co. Wicklow was to benefit from this development on a number of fronts, particularly in health care, when diseases such as TB and polio almost disappeared.

By the late 1960s extensive improvements to Wicklow Harbour facilitated an improvement in the import and export trade. There was a viable trade in the export of livestock, particularly sheep and cattle. Timber from Co. Wicklow forests was exported, along with general cargoes from the many new factories being established in the region. The Goulding plant, manufacturing agricultural fertilisers, was an important industry in the town. Veha Radiators also began production, employing more than a hundred workers.

In 1965 the Minister for Industry and Commerce established Nítrigin Éireann (NET) to operate a nitrogenous fertiliser factory in Arklow. The factory went into production with a work force of 1,250; a subsidiary company, Arklow Gypsum, operated a plaster and plasterboard factory at North Quay, employing a hundred people. A large jetty was built at Arklow Rock to accommodate larger ships exporting granite from the Parnell Quarries.

The best-known shipbuilders in Arklow were John Tyrrell and Sons. In 1966 James Tyrrell, Michael Tyrrell, and Victor Hall established Arklow Shipping as a co-operative for the eight ships owned by them. There followed a steady expansion, with new and larger ships being commissioned. The company subsequently re-registered its ships in the Netherlands, and today there are very few ships registered in Ireland.

In 1969 mining was to reappear in Avoca when Discovery Mines of Canada reopened the abandoned mines, and up to five hundred workers were employed there.

In the late 1960s Newcastle Hospital reopened as a residential home for psychiatric patients.

From the late 1960s construction commenced on several large private estates in the Bray area, including Ardmore.

The 1970s

The census of 1971 recorded an increase of 6,000 in the population of the county in five years. During this period the Rathdown area, including Enniskerry, Greystones, and Delgany, showed the greatest growth, because of its close proximity to Dublin. In two decades, 1950–70, the number of marriages in the county increased by half, leading to a demand for more housing.

In 1972 Shelton Abbey near Arklow was transferred to the Department of Justice for use as a detention centre for young offenders.

In 1973 the ESB opened a 292-megawatt pumped-storage station at Turlough Hill, at the summit of the Wicklow Gap above Glendalough. This is the only pumped-storage hydro-electric station in Ireland. Each night, when demand for electricity is low, the waters of Lough Nahanagan are pumped to the reservoir on top of Turlough Hill; from there they are released during the day to drive the turbines, deep inside the mountain.

With the worldwide slump in demand for nylon products, Industrial Yarns experienced serious trading difficulties from the mid-1970s, and the work force was drastically reduced. In 1977 the German computer firm Nixdorf opened its plant on the Boghall Road in Bray, but the company later experienced financial difficulties and closed the plant.

On 5 October 1977 the founder and chairman of the Irish Republican Socialist Party, Séamus Costello, was murdered in Dublin by the Official IRA. He was born in Bray and in 1967 was elected an independent member of Wicklow County Council.

The 1980s

Between 1980 and 1985 Wicklow County Council built 977 houses throughout the county. In 1982 Avoca Mines closed for the last time, and the remaining workers were made redundant; all that was left of a once-thriving industry were the remains of chimneystacks and huge mounds of mine waste.

In July 1984 the Dublin Area Rapid transit (DART) electric suburban railway went into service, linking Bray with Howth by way of Dublin. By 1986 Co. Wicklow was the most urbanised of the counties surrounding Dublin, having 56 per cent of its population living in towns with a population of 1,500 or more.

On the night of 26 August 1986 the east coast was struck by a devastating storm, known as Hurricane Charlie. Co. Wicklow was particularly badly hit, with extensive damage caused to many boats, bridges, and roads. Some minor roads suffered severe flooding and were impassable; Bailey bridges were used to temporarily replace those seriously damaged or destroyed. The Dargle River burst its banks, causing serious flooding in Little Bray and in sea-front areas. The bridge in Annamoe, originally built in 1746, was the subject of controversy when it was struck in the storm. A Bailey bridge was constructed until a new bridge was erected that gives a wide entrance to the village. Repair work in the county continued into the 1990s.

In 1987 the County Wicklow Heritage Society was founded with the support of the County Development Team, and a genealogical project covering the county was also begun.

The 1990s

Throughout Co. Wicklow the newly built industrial estates attracted a number of industries. The most notable were A. O. Smith, De La Rue Smurfit, and Schering-Plough, with operations in Bray and Rathdrum. Nypro, Solus Teo., and Lithographic Universal were big employers in the Bray area. Kerry Foods in Shillelagh and Holfeld Plastics in Kilmacanogue gave employment in those rural communities.

In 1990 Maxtor took over the Nixdorf plant in Bray, but this company also closed after a number of years. Later the computer giant Dell opened its sales and support offices on the site and quickly became a major employer. Woodfab and Avoca Handweavers continue to give significant employment in Co. Wicklow.

In the past two decades local communities have become more aware of heritage and archaeological sites in their areas. In 1991 Greystones community organisations were successful in having a proposed housing scheme on a mediaeval settlement at Rathdown, on the southern slope of Bray Head, rejected by An Bord Pleanála. In other parts of the county, road works have been delayed because of new archaeological finds. Perhaps the most controversial decision by An Bord Pleanála was when it halted work in progress on a proposed visitors' centre at Luggala in 1995. The Office of Public Works planned the centre for the Wicklow National Park, but An Bord Pleanála rejected this on the grounds that it would lead to an unacceptable degradation of the area's fragile ecology and landscape. The extra traffic that would be generated on the narrow roads, together with the obligatory car parks, was a determining factor.

In the early hours of Tuesday 19 March 1996, 54-year-old Tom Nevin, joint proprietor of Jack White's Inn in Brittas Bay, was shot dead in the kitchen of his pub while counting the day's takings. His wife, Catherine Nevin, was found gagged by the Gardaí; she told them she had heard two cars driving away. On 14 April 1997 Catherine Nevin was charged with the murder of her husband and with conspiring to have him murdered. Her trial began on 12 January 2000 in the Central Criminal Court but collapsed on 26 January when the jury were overheard deliberating. A second trial was also aborted when one member of the jury became ill. A third trial began on 14 February 2000, at which three men gave evidence that they were solicited by Catherine Nevin to murder her husband. The jury's deliberations lasted for five days. Finally, on 14 April 1997, after sixty-one days and three trials, Catherine Nevin was found guilty of the murder of her husband and conspiring to have him murdered and was sentenced to life imprisonment.

In the past decade Wicklow County Council and the town councils of Bray, Arklow, Wicklow, and Greystones (renamed town councils in 2002) have undertaken ambitious sewerage and road schemes. The first new road to be completed was the Newtownmountkennedy Bypass, east of the village, drawing much of the traffic away from narrow roads. The following year the opening of the Shankill–Bray Bypass helped to ease the constant traffic congestion in Bray. In 1991 improvements to the N11 road at the Glen of the Downs ran into a series of problems. To enable the stretch of road from Kilmacanogue to the Glen of the Downs to be developed into a dual carriageway, it was planned to fell trees in

Bellevue Wood, a woodland of native trees. Environmental activists were outraged and waged a campaign of protest and opposition. Some protesters encamped in trees on each side of the road to prevent the council felling them. They were brought before the courts on a number of occasions, and a protracted dispute followed. Finally, in 1999, Wicklow County Council began felling the trees, and the protesters reluctantly departed. The same year the Arklow bypass was opened, shortening the road journey time between Dublin and Rosslare. Other road improvements included the Southern Cross Road in Bray, on land acquired from Lord Meath, and the N81 road in west Wicklow.

New sewerage works have been undertaken in Bray, Greystones, Arklow, and Wicklow. In recent years many towns and villages have benefited from urban and village renewal schemes; historic buildings and heritage centres have been renovated and amenities improved.

Despite the economic boom of the 1990s, industry in Co. Wicklow suffered a number of setbacks. The Japanese company Noritake acquired the Arklow Pottery plant, but the company ran into financial difficulties, and a liquidator was appointed in August 1998. The following April, production at the plant ceased.

Large-scale engineering works were undertaken to extend the DART line through the tunnels under Bray Head. The growing population of Greystones and Kilcoole had lobbied for this service, which opened in 2001.

The twenty-first century

In 2001 a retreat centre comprising five 'cillíns' or hermitages was opened in the grounds of St Kevin's Church, Glendalough. These single-accommodation hermitages were built to provide a solitary retreat for those wishing to take time off from the pressures of contemporary life.

In 2001 Wicklow port recorded a significant throughput of 171,448 tonnes, an increase of 13 per cent on the previous year. In 2002 a study suggested that the port was capable of handling up to four times its present commercial business.

The Newtownmountkennedy to Ballinabarny Road Improvement Scheme is the penultimate section of the N11 road in Co. Wicklow to be upgraded to national standard. The final project will be the Rathnew–Arklow road improvement scheme. On its completion, the county will have a dual carriageway from Bray to Arklow.

In 2002 there was bad news for the workers of the IFI fertiliser plant in Arklow. Management announced that the 551 workers employed in Arklow, Cork, and Belfast were to be made redundant with the closure of the plant.

Over the coming years the horizon off the Arklow coast will be transformed with the construction of the world's largest offshore wind farm. Two hundred giant turbines for generating electricity, 260 feet (80 metres) high, will be installed on a sandbank 4 miles (7 kilometres) off the coast.

12 FAMOUS LINKS *with* CO. WICKLOW

OSCAR WILDE

ONE OF IRELAND'S most colourful and most controversial literary figures, Oscar Wilde, had family connections with Bray. During the development of the town his father, Sir William Wilde, a prominent surgeon, had built five houses on the sea front–numbers 1–4 Esplanade Terrace, and Elsinore. It is said that his wife had Oscar and Willie christened in the small church in Glencree.

In 1864, when Wilde was knighted, the family were socially and financially secure, but he was to become involved in a scandal. He had had love affairs with various women, but one of them, a patient named Mary Travers, was not discreet about their relationship. When Wilde ended the affair she sent a series of anonymous letters to his wife, describing him as a spiteful old lunatic. She claimed he had interfered with her while she was his patient, and she produced a pamphlet to ensure that her allegations became widely known.

Wilde's wife took the children–Willie, Oscar, and Isola–to Esplanade Terrace to avoid the scandal. But she was allowed no peace, as Travers sent out boys selling the pamphlet at her door. Lady Wilde wrote an angry letter to the girl's father, who was professor of medical jurisprudence at Trinity College, Dublin, complaining of his daughter's actions. Miss Travers came across the letter and sued Lady Wilde for libel. She claimed £2,000 damages, knowing that Wilde would be cited as co-defendant.

The jury assessed the damages at a farthing; but the publicity had an unfortunate effect on Wilde, whose health rapidly deteriorated. He died in 1876, when Oscar was in his second year at the University of Oxford. Oscar inherited the property in Bray, but because of his father's complex financial affairs he was forced to sell the houses. He received less than £3,000 for them, most of which he lost in court cases over confused contracts.

After an illustrious artistic and literary career, Wilde was later tried on charges of sodomy, convicted, and was imprisoned for two years. He died in Paris in 1900.

SHERIDAN LE FANU

In the middle of the nineteenth century many of the Le Fanu family lived in north Co. Wicklow. The most renowned member of the family was the novelist Joseph Sheridan Le Fanu, a grandnephew of the writer Richard Brinsley Sheridan. Le Fanu was to make his reputation with novels of mystery and the supernatural. He was born in Dublin in 1814 and was called to the bar but gave up a career in law to become a writer. His *Authentic Narrative of a Haunted House* (1862) described a summer resort to which the narrator and his wife retired as invalids. Illness and convalescence were recurring themes in his writing.

During the first ten years of their marriage Sheridan Le Fanu and his wife, Susan, spent prolonged periods in Bray and Kingstown (Dún Laoghaire)—either of which would fit the description in *An Authentic Narrative*. During the time he was writing *Uncle Silas* he was also absorbed in his own family history, but he was struck by illness. In 1864 he spent a long period in Bray recovering from bronchitis. His gothic novels include *The Cook and the Anchor* (1845), *The Tenants of Malo* (1867), and *In a Glass Darkly* (1872). Following the death of his wife he became withdrawn and broke off contact with even his closest friends. He died in 1873. W. R. Le Fanu, Sheridan's younger brother, lived at Summerhill, Enniskerry. He wrote *Seventy Years of Irish Life*, a book full of anecdotes and reminiscences, in which Bray and the Dargle are mentioned.

JAMES JOYCE

One of the most famous residents of Bray was the writer James Joyce. In May 1887 his father, John Joyce, took the family to live at number 1 Martello Terrace, a fashionable three-storey house, so close to the sea that the area in front of the house was frequently flooded. In number 4 Martello Terrace lived James Vance, who ran two pharmacies in the town, and the families became friends. The Vances' eldest daughter, four months younger than James, was an attractive girl named Eileen. James's aunt, Dante, warned him that if he played with Eileen (who was a Protestant) he would definitely go to Hell. The town was full of young women, those 'seaside girls' that remained in Joyce's memory for many years, to surface in *Ulysses.*

Joyces's singing voice was good enough for him to join his parents in an amateur concert at Bray Boat Club on 26 June 1888, when he was six. He was an adventurous child; at the age of seven he rode his tricycle from the outskirts of Dublin to visit a nurse, while his distraught parents searched for him. In September 1888 he became a boarder at Clongowes Wood College, Co. Kildare, but he enjoyed his visits home to see his family and Eileen Vance.

In 1891 John Joyce's financial problems increased, and the family were forced to leave Bray and withdraw James from Clongowes Wood. The house in Martello Terrace was the setting for the Christmas dinner scene in *Portrait of the Artist as a Young Man,* when the father and a family friend argue over the betrayal of Parnell.

In 1904 Joyce and his wife, Nora Barnacle, left Dublin and settled in Trieste, where Joyce taught English while writing *Dubliners* and *A Portrait of the Artist as a Young Man.* In 1922 *Ulysses* was published; it was greeted with controversy but was later to be considered a masterpiece. Joyce was never again to visit Bray, but in 1935 his daughter, Lucia, who was introverted and spent long spells in mental institutions, accompanied his sister Eileen to her home in Bray.

JOHN MILLINGTON SYNGE

The playwright John Millington Synge, the youngest of a family of eight, was born in 1871 in Rathfarnham, Co. Dublin. He was a quiet and shy boy with a keen interest in nature. His connections with Co. Wicklow began in his childhood when he travelled daily to Aravon School in Bray from his home in Orwell Park and later by train from Kingstown. He was a popular boy and particularly enjoyed swimming in Naylor's Cove with his classmates. Each summer his mother moved the entire household to Greystones, then a fishing village, or to Annamoe, where they rented a house. The family returned every year to Co. Wicklow until John was twenty-one.

While he socialised with the family, Synge also turned his attention to writing. With his highly tuned curiosity he observed the people and the countryside. Walking and cycling the roads, he would stop to chat with tramps and tradesmen, recording their stories and unusual phrases in his notebook. He was a constant source of anxiety to his family. His mother, who mixed socially only with members of her own religion and class, was also disturbed with his loss of faith, as many of her relatives were clergymen.

Synge drew on his experiences among the country people of Co. Wicklow for the ingredients of his plays, some of which were set in the county; *The Tinker's Wedding, The Well of the Saints, When the Moon Has Set,* and *The Shadow of the Glen* include references to Arklow, Kilquade, Rathdrum, and Ballinaclash.

On 26 January 1907, when Synge's play *The Playboy of the Western World* was staged in the Abbey Theatre, Dublin, it caused a riot. W. B. Yeats went on stage to quell the uproar and to support Synge's work. The play was to become widely recognised as a masterpiece and was an important factor in the Irish literary revival. Synge died on 24 March 1909.

ROBERT HALPIN

Robert Halpin, who laid the first transatlantic cable, was born in Wicklow on 16 February 1836. His father, James Halpin, ran the Bridge House, a dockside tavern, a favourite haunt of both sailors and dockers. Robert began his seafaring career at the age of eleven when he joined a coasting vessel. He rose quickly to officer rank and in 1855 transferred from sail to steam and was given command of Atlantic mail ships. In 1866 he served as navigation officer on the *Great Eastern,* then the largest ship in the world. He was promoted to captain of the *Great Eastern* and succeeded in completing the laying of the Atlantic cable between Valencia Island, Co. Kerry, and Heart's Content, Newfoundland, on which the first successful transoceanic telegraph message was transmitted. In 1869 he successfully laid what was then the longest underwater cable, from Brest to Newfoundland.

In 1880 Halpin built a mansion, Tinnakilly House, at Rathnew and retired there. An infected toenail led to gangrene, causing his death on 20 January 1894 at the age of fifty-seven. He was buried in the family vault on Church Hill, Wicklow town.

PAUL HENRY

The artist Paul Henry, born in Belfast in 1876, lived in many houses around Bray in the later years of his life, most notably at number 1 Sidmonton Square. As a young man he was influenced by Whistler and the post-impressionists. He was best known for his evocative oil paintings of the rugged scenery and personalities of the west of Ireland, particularly Achill Island. He designed a poster, 'Connemara Landscape', for the London, Midland, and Scottish Railway that became the biggest-selling poster of the time.

Though he was red-green colour-blind, Henry was a prolific artist who had almost fifty international exhibitions. In 1945 he lost his sight completely, and he came to live in Bray. In 1951 his autobiography, *An Irish Portrait,* was published. His first wife, Grace Mitchell, also a well-known artist, died in 1953. Henry died on 24 August 1958, and he is buried in St Patrick's graveyard, Enniskerry.

DESMOND FITZGERALD

In 1915, when Desmond FitzGerald, a leader in the Irish Volunteers, was stationed at Dingle, Co. Kerry, the British authorities instructed him to leave the area within six days. He was forbidden to live in Dublin, but an area from Bray to Dublin was permitted to him. As a result of a legacy the family was financially secure, and they moved to live in Bray in Fairyhill House, a large house in Killarney Road consisting of three acres of gardens and thirteen acres of farmland. Desmond's wife, Mabel, was secretary to George Bernard Shaw.

Arthur Griffith gave FitzGerald a list of potential Volunteers in the area, and he set about forming a company, recruiting and training them in the Wicklow Mountains. He also arranged a large meeting in favour of home rule in Bray at which Michael O'Rahilly was one of the main speakers. When Desmond ventured into Dublin on a bicycle he was arrested for breaking restrictions. He was found guilty and sentenced to imprisonment in Mountjoy Jail but on 31 March 1916 was released, in time to join the rising in the GPO. He escaped capture and made his way back to Bray by way of the mountains but was arrested, court-martialled, and sentenced to life imprisonment. The sentence was later commuted to twenty years' imprisonment. In the Cumann na nGaedheal government of 1923 he was appointed Minister for External Affairs. He died on 19 April 1947.

GARRET FITZGERALD

One of Desmond FitzGerald's children, Garret, was to follow his father's footsteps into politics. Garret spent the formative years of his life in Bray, from the age of two to eleven. He attended St Brigid's School in Quinsborough Road, where for a time he was the only boy in a class of girls. His parents were extremely sociable, and most weekends the house was full of people, who came to enjoy walks and tennis. The constant flow of visitors, who included W. B. Yeats, Jacques Maritain, T. S. Eliot, Ernest Blythe, and Lord Longford, made a lasting impression on Garret. From constant outings with his governess, Miss Cuddy, he came to know every road and laneway from the Great Sugar Loaf to Enniskerry and the Scalp. Frequently, when not accompanied by an adult, he would explore Lord Meath's estate at Kilruddery.

In March 1937 the FitzGeralds sold Fairyhill House and left Bray. Garret went on to become a prominent economist, Government minister, and finally Taoiseach. It was appropriate that he should officially open the Bray Heritage Centre on 8 July 1985.

SEÁN T. O'KELLY

Three Presidents of Ireland have had strong ties with Co. Wicklow. The first was Seán T. O'Kelly, who was born in Dublin on 25 August 1882. He was a veteran of the 1916 Rising and a founder-member of Fianna Fáil in 1926. He was returned to the first Dáil Éireann, where he became Ceann Comhairle on 21 January 1919. After rejecting the Treaty he supported the republicans during the Civil War, after which he was Sinn Féin envoy to the United States. He served in a number of ministerial posts, including Local Government and Public Health, and Finance, and as Tánaiste (Deputy Prime Minister).

In 1939 O'Kelly came to live in Roundwood Park, Roundwood, and he was living there when Fianna Fáil nominated him as its candidate in the 1945 presidential election. He defeated Seán Mac Eoin to become the second President of Ireland, succeeding Dr Douglas Hyde. In 1952 he was re-elected unopposed. He retired in June 1959 and moved back to Roundwood. He died on 23 November 1966, aged eighty-four.

ERSKINE CHILDERS

Erskine Hamilton Childers, son of the author and patriot Robert Erskine Childers, was born in London on 11 December 1905. In 1914 Erskine Childers senior, author of the best-selling book *The Riddle of the Sands*, brought arms into Howth on board the *Asgard*. He opposed the Anglo-Irish Treaty and was arrested at his home in Annamoe. In 1922 when he was court-martialled and sentenced to death he shook hands with each member of the firing-squad.

The young Erskine Childers spent much of his childhood holidays at Glendalough House, Annamoe. He attended Trinity College and the University of Cambridge and then became advertising manager of the *Irish Press*. In 1938 he was elected to Dáil Éireann for Fianna Fáil, and over a political career of thirty-five years he held many ministerial posts, including Posts and Telegraphs, Lands, and Transport and Power, as well as the post of Tánaiste. In 1973 he was elected to succeed Éamon de Valera as fourth President of Ireland. He died suddenly on 17 November 1974 and is buried in Derrylossary cemetery, close to the family home.

CEARBHALL Ó DÁLAIGH

On 12 February 1911 Cearbhall Ó Dálaigh, who was to become the fifth President of Ireland, was born at 85 Main Street, Bray, the second son of the manager of a fish and poultry shop. His mother had been active in the national movement, and following the 1916 Rising she was arrested by the RIC. In 1915 Cearbhall was enrolled in Loreto Convent, Bray, but the mother superior asked his mother to withdraw him after the first day, as he was too young. Three years later he became a pupil at Big Bray's National School, Herbert Road. He was always proud of his association with Bray's oldest educational establishment. For a time the family lived at 3 Old Court Terrace, Vevay Road. When Cearbhall was thirteen his father died, and the family moved to Dublin.

Ó Dálaigh became a barrister and carved out a distinguished career in Ireland and on the Continent; he served as Attorney-General, Chief Justice, President of the Supreme Court, and a judge of the Court of Justice of the European Communities. In 1974 he became an agreed candidate of the three main parties for the Presidency of Ireland, and he was returned unopposed, to succeed Erskine Childers. When as President he referred two bills (the Criminal Law Jurisdiction Bill and Emergency Powers Bill) to the Supreme Court he was referred to as 'a thundering disgrace' by the Minister for Defence, Patrick Donegan. When no disciplinary action was taken against Donegan by the Taoiseach, Liam Cosgrave, Ó Dálaigh resigned on 22 October 1976. He died on 21 March 1978 and was buried near Sneem, Co. Kerry.

13 The ARTS

The VALLEY OF WRITERS

IN 1969 THE Minister for Finance, Charles Haughey, sponsored a law that gave tax exemptions to writers and artists living in Ireland. This resulted in a significant number of writers taking up residence in the country, and particularly in Co. Wicklow, which came to be known as the 'Valley of the Writers'. One of these, the thriller-writer Alistair MacLean, best known for *The Guns of Navarone* and *When Eight Bells Toll,* maintained a low profile for the duration of his stay in Violet Hill, Bray; he left Co. Wicklow in 1979. The best-selling author Frederick Forsythe, author of *The Day of the Jackal* and *The Odessa File,* lived in Kilgarron House, Enniskerry. The science-fiction writer Anne McCaffrey, of the Dragonquest series, lived in Kilquade; Morgan Llewellyn, author of *Brian Boru,* lived in Newcastle; and the prolific Gordon Thomas lived in Ashford, as did Peter de Rosa. Gerard Seymour, John Gardiner, and John Clive lived in Delgany.

FILMS

Since the early 1920s Co. Wicklow has provided a backdrop for film-makers. Billy Power, a barber from Bray, was one of the earliest film pioneers. With the assistance of a local drama group he wrote and directed his first feature, *Rosaleen Dhu* (1919), and his barber shop doubled as a laboratory for developing film. In 1920, while filming his second feature, *An Irish Vendetta,* he was thrown from his horse, and he died later from his injuries.

One of the most notable films was Laurence Olivier's *Henry V,* shot in Powerscourt in 1943, with hundreds of extras hired to play English and French soldiers. During the 1950s Powerscourt Demesne saw the pounding of hooves in two swashbuckling films, *Knights of the Round Table* (1953), starring Rock Hudson, and *Captain Lightfoot* (1954), starring Robert Taylor. Powerscourt Waterfall was chosen for a sequence in *Moby Dick* (1955) with Gregory Peck.

One of the biggest boosts to film-making in Ireland occurred in 1958, when Ireland's first film studio, Ardmore Studios, opened in Bray. This was a fully serviced studio that could facilitate productions of any size. The first films to be made there were based on Abbey Theatre plays and included *Home Is the Hero* (1959) with Arthur Kennedy, *The Big Birthday* (1959) with Barry Fitzgerald, and *Sally's Irish Rogue* (1960) with Julie Harris. *Shake Hands with the Devil* (1959), starring James Cagney, was the first major film to be shot in Ardmore; this was followed by *A Terrible Beauty* (1960), with Robert Mitchum.

In the mid-1960s a number of dramatic films of note were shot in Bray, including a controversial film called *The Mark* (1961), starring Stuart Whitman as a man released from prison after serving a sentence for child abuse. *Term of Trial* (1961) was a tense drama set in an English school starring Laurence Olivier. The great America director Francis Ford Coppola, who later made *The Godfather* (1972), directed his first film in Co. Wicklow. *The Haunted and the Hunted* (1963), also known as *Dementia 13,* was shot in three weeks–two weeks in Ardmore and one week on location in Newtownmountkennedy. Laurence Harvey featured in *The Running Man* (1963), made in Co. Wicklow by Carol Reed, and with Kim Novak in a remake of *Of Human Bondage* (1964).

John Huston, who was keen to foster an Irish film industry, directed three films in Co. Wicklow: *The List of Adrian Messenger* (1963), *Sinful Davey* (1969), and *The Mackintosh Man* (1973). Richard Burton was highly praised for his role as a seedy spy in *The Spy Who Came In from the Cold* (1964). For *The Blue Max* (1965), areas of Co. Wicklow were skilfully transformed to re-create the Battle of the Somme. The film, which starred George Peppard and James Mason, used several hundred Irish soldiers for the battle scenes, while fighter-planes staged dogfights over Callary Bog. Peter O'Toole and Katharine Hepburn made an excellent team in *The Lion in Winter* (1968). Each morning before reporting to Ardmore, Hepburn would take a swim in the sea at Bray. Other big films produced in Ardmore were *Flight of the Doves* (1971), *Images* (1972), directed by Robert Altman, with Ron Moody, and *The First Great Train Robbery* (1979), an action yarn starring Seán Connery.

In 1973 John Boorman directed *Zardoz,* a futuristic film also starring Connery, on location in the Wicklow Mountains. Some years later Boorman followed this with *Excalibur* (1980), based on the legend of King Arthur, for which elaborate sets were constructed in Ardmore and around Co. Wicklow. In the 1990s Boorman was to direct an impressive black-and-white film, *The General* (1997), based on the life of the Dublin criminal Martin Cahill, which won him an award at the Cannes Film Festival. Boorman, like John Huston, became deeply involved in offering his expertise to boost the Irish film industry.

One of America's leading directors, Stanley Kubrick, chose many locations in Ireland for shooting *Barry Lyndon* (1974), a lavish film set in the eighteenth century. Powerscourt House and grounds featured prominently in the film, which starred Ryan O'Neal and Hardy Kruger. Half way through the shooting Kubrick suddenly left the country; it was alleged that he had received a threat from the IRA. In 1991 Kilruddery House was to feature in *Far and Away,* with Tom Cruise and Nicole Kidman. The spectacular scenery of the Featherbeds and the Sally Gap areas of the Wicklow Mountains have featured in a score of films, including *When Harry Became a Tree* (1999), *Evelyn* (2001) with Pierce Brosnan, *Cal* (1984), *Into the West* (1991) with Gabriel Byrne, *Moondance* (1993), *Dancing at Lughnasa* (1997) with Meryl Streep, and *Ordinary Decent Criminal* (1998) with Kevin Spacey.

Over the last two decades two Irish directors, Neil Jordan and Jim Sheridan, have had strong connections with Co. Wicklow. Jordan, who shot part of his debut film, *Angel* (1981), in Bray, lived in Martello Terrace for a number of years. His film *The Miracle* (1990), starring Dónal McCann, was set entirely in Bray. He won an Academy Award for his screenplay for *The Crying Game* (1992), shot enormous crowd scenes for *Michael Collins* in Bray and Rathdrum, and filmed on the Featherbeds for

The Butcher Boy (1997). Kilruddery House and St Kevin's Square in Bray featured prominently in Jim Sheridan's debut film, *My Left Foot* (1988). Daniel Day-Lewis won an Academy Award for his role as the disabled writer Christy Brown; Brenda Fricker also won an Academy Award for her part as his mother. Sequences for Sheridan's films *The Boxer* (1997) and *In America* (2001) were filmed in Ardmore Studios. Another director whose work has been critically acclaimed in recent years is Paddy Breathnach, a native of Bray, who directed *Ailsa* (1993), *I Went Down* (1995), and *Blow Dry* (1999).

Members of the Defence Forces donned a variety of uniforms for the battle scenes in Mel Gibson's *Braveheart* (1994) and Steven Spielberg's *Saving Private Ryan* (1997). Gibson starred in and directed *Braveheart,* and its bloody battle scenes were enacted at the Curragh and near Manor Kilbride. The film won five Academy Awards, including those for best film and best director.

Numerous other films have been shot on location in Co. Wicklow, including *Oliver Twist* (1995), *The Commitments* (1991), *Space Truckers* (1995), *Moll Flanders* (1996), *Saint Patrick* (1997), *Agnes Brown* (1998), *Angela's Ashes* (1997), *Disco Pigs* (2000), *Not Afraid* (2000), *Reign of Fire* (2001), *Bloody Sunday* (2001), *The Count of Monte Cristo* (2000), *Dark Eagle* (2002), *Ella Enchanted* (2002), *Veronica Guerin* (2002), and *King Arthur* (2003). The Wicklow Film Commission endeavours to entice new film productions to the county, for which lucrative tax concessions are available.

GLENROE AND BALLYKISSANGEL

Two of Co. Wicklow's most famous villages are not to be found on the map. Thousands of visitors come annually on the trail of the fictional villages of Glenroe and Ballykissangel. Over the last thirty years Co. Wicklow has been the location for three popular television series. The first was 'Bracken', created by Wesley Burrowes. The setting was a farming community, and the series starred Niall Tóibín, Dana Wynter, Joe Lynch, and Mick Lally. When 'Bracken' finished, in the early 1980s, Lynch and Lally became pivotal characters as Dinny and Miley Byrne in a new rural series, 'Glenroe', also developed by Wesley Burrowes. It was filmed in Kilcoole, and since then many business premises in the village have been named after characters from the series.

Avoca, Co. Wicklow, gained fame as the fictional Ballykissangel in the BBC television series of the same name. The series, created by Kieran Prenderville, was based on the arrival of an English priest in an Irish village. Despite the departure of Stephen Tompkinson (Father Peter) and Derval Kirwan (Assumpta), the series continued equally successfully with a number of Irish actors, including Bosco Hogan, Tina Kelleher, Niall Tóibín, and Owen Roe. Many local people were employed as extras, and the community gained from the thousands of tourists who visited the village.

ARTS AND CULTURE

Co. Wicklow has a history of strong cultural and artistic activity extending back for centuries. In 1825 Walter Scott wrote an account of a visit to the open-air theatre in Kilruddery. Oscar Wilde, Sir William Wilde, John Millington Synge, and James Joyce all had links with Co. Wicklow, and aspects of the county appear in the works of the latter two.

For many decades Co. Wicklow has had a strong tradition of social history, with historical societies in Wicklow, Greystones, Arklow, Kilmacanogue, Enniskerry, Roundwood, Baltinglass, and Bray. Their journals and lectures are a valuable asset to members and to those researching a diverse range of topics in the county's heritage and history. The county also has an abundance of arts and writers' groups, many of which have produced published poets and authors.

Since 1973 the County Development Office has administered grants to historical societies, community groups, and artists' and drama groups to help them promote cultural events. In 1997 an arts officer was appointed for the county. A recent feature of the social calendar of the county has been the introduction of summer schools and autumn schools. The Synge Summer School, held each July in Rathdrum, presents readings and lectures on the works of the playwright. In August in nearby Avondale House a series of speakers contributes to the Parnell Summer School. The Oscar Wilde Autumn School, held in Bray, commemorates the anniversary of Wilde's death in October with lectures by academics and literary figures. Other important events in Co. Wicklow include Dunlavin Arts Festival and Music Under the Mountains.

Over the past twenty years many writers, directors, singers, actors, and painters have lived in Co. Wicklow. The writers James Plunkett, Clare Boylan, Joan O'Neill, Peter Regan, James Douglas, Bernard Farrell, Hugh Carr, Cathy Kelly, Liz McManus, Lee Dunne, Mary Rose Callaghan, and Wesley Burrowes. Colm Wilkinson, who lived in Bray, represented Ireland in the 1978 Eurovision Song Contest and later embarked on a singing career, most notably with *Les Misérables*. Paddy Moloney of the Chieftains, the long-established folk music group, lives in Annamoe. Phil Coulter, the composer, singer, pianist, and record producer, also lives in Bray. Another resident of Bray is the blues and folk singer Mary Coughlan.

For many years the film actress Dana Wynter lived in a cottage at Glenmacnass. The actor Daniel Day-Lewis bought nearby Castlekevin and lives there with his wife, the writer-director Rebecca Miller. Other actors who have lived in the county include Paddy Dawson, Niall O'Brien, Éamonn Morrissey, Frank O'Keeffe, and Hazel O'Connor. Chris de Burgh, the singer and songwriter, lives in Enniskerry. Bono (Paul Hewson) of U2 lived for a number of years in the martello tower above Bray Harbour; Spanish students occasionally stole underwear from his clothes line as a souvenir. The documentary and wildlife film maker, Éamon de Buitléar, lived for most of his life beside the River Dargle in Bray. The poet Seamus Heaney lived for a time in Ashford, and his fellow-poet Thomas Kinsella at Glenmacnass. The Breton artist Yann Renard Goulet lived for many years in Bray.

Despite endless campaigns for many decades, Co. Wicklow had to wait until 2002 for its first purpose-built municipal arts centre, eventually opened in Bray. Concerts and professional and amateur productions had to be staged in parochial halls and school gyms. Now there is a new centre, known as the Mermaid, which includes a 242-seat auditorium.

14 TOURISM *and* SPORT

FROM THE MIDDLE of the nineteenth century Co. Wicklow has been a popular resort because of its diverse scenery, evident from Arklow Rock to Bray Head, from Carnew through the mountains and glens to the lakes at Blessington. The county is a place of great architectural set-pieces, with a necklace of splendid country houses, castles, and vast estates dating from the Middle Ages. Five of the country's leading heritage gardens are in Co. Wicklow: Kilruddery House and Gardens (Bray), Powerscourt House and Gardens (Enniskerry), Mount Usher Gardens (Ashford), Avondale House and Forest Park (Rathdrum), and Russborough House (Blessington).

From the early years of the twentieth century the county's coastal resorts, such as Bray, Wicklow, and Arklow, became very popular, but with a poor transport system most of the inland beauty spots were inaccessible to visitors. One of these was Glendalough, but in 1927 St Kevin's Bus Service began, linking it with Dublin. St Kevin's Bus Service still runs a daily service, carrying tourists, workers, and shoppers.

From the 1940s, changing trends had a detrimental effect on the reputation of Bray as a holiday resort: it was to deteriorate from being considered the Brighton of Ireland to being the Blackpool of Ireland, with big dance-halls, amusement arcades, fish-and-chip shops, and singing pubs. The Arcadia Ballroom became one of the most popular dancing venues in the country, attracting vast crowds every weekend; bands such as those of Mick Del and Billy Carter became household names, while the later showband era brought the Royal, Capitol, Miami, and Dixies to the ballroom. Roy Orbison, Kenny Ball, and Acker Bilk were among the visiting international acts to perform at the Arcadia. Other popular dancing venues of the period were the Eagle's Nest and the Bar B.

For two decades following the Second World War there was an influx of visitors from England, Scotland, and Wales who spent their annual holidays in Bray. Hotels and guesthouses were filled to capacity for three months, and a broad spectrum of house-owners opened their homes for the lucrative bed-and-breakfast trade.

From the mid-1960s there was a noticeable drop in the number of tourists to Bray and the other coastal towns. A number of factors contributed to this decline: cheap air travel, package holidays, an increasing car population, the car ferry at Dún Laoghaire, and rising prices. But in other parts of the county the trend was in the opposite direction, and the number of visitors increased significantly. Powerscourt, Russborough, Kilruddery, and Mount Usher became more accessible to visitors with their own transport.

The country has always depended on tourist income, which now amounts to approximately €36 million annually from day-trippers and €43 million from longer stays in hotels and guesthouses. Wicklow County Tourism promotes tourism and enterprise in the county.

POWERSCOURT HOUSE AND GARDENS

Powerscourt House and Gardens, just above Enniskerry at the foothills of the Wicklow Mountains, is one of the most frequently-visited gardens in the country. In 1730 the great Palladian mansion was designed by the renowned German architect Richard Cassells, incorporating parts of an ancient castle. In 1745 Viscount Powerscourt began work on the extensive gardens, laid out among spectacular mountains, lakes, and forests. The gardens have a combination of long terraces, ornate lakes, walks, and walled gardens and a vast array of trees, plants, and shrubs. In 1974 the house was destroyed by fire, but it has since been partly restored. It has now been renovated, and also houses a restaurant and shops.

RUSSBOROUGH HOUSE, BLESSINGTON

In 1740 the prosperous Dublin brewer Joseph Leeson inherited his father's fortune and decided to build a mansion befitting a member of Parliament and man of wealth. He also commissioned Richard Cassells to design a house in the Palladian style. In 1952 Sir Alfred Beit bought the house as a home for his art collection, and in 1976 he set up a foundation and opened the house to the public. Russborough House has an excellent international art collection, consisting of Dutch, Flemish, and Spanish masterpieces, as well as displays of silver, bronze, fine furniture, tapestries, and porcelain. Adjoining the house are lakes and extensive woodlands.

AVONDALE HOUSE AND FOREST PARK

Avondale House, south of Rathdrum, is the birthplace of Charles Stewart Parnell (1846–1891). Samuel Hayes built the Georgian house in 1779 on the banks of the Avonmore River. In 1904 the property was acquired by the state, and extensive repairs were made. Avondale, which attracts more than 100,000 visitors annually, is also the cradle of modern Irish forestry and contains a forest park of 530 acres (215 hectares), with an enormous variety of trees to be seen along its roads and woodland paths. The house is open to the public, and there is also a restaurant and a picnic area.

WICKLOW GAOL

In 1986 the first steps were taken by Wicklow County Council to restore Wicklow Gaol, built in the early eighteenth century to house criminals and 'rebels'. In 1998 it was opened as a tourist attraction. A variety of media–audio, graphics, actors, and figures–gives a flavour of the political and social history of prison life. Visitors are guided through the gaol by actors portraying the gaoler, a 1798 insurgent, and a ship's captain. The Wicklow Genealogical Research Centre is also based in the gaol.

KILRUDDERY HOUSE AND GARDENS

Kilruddery House, on the outskirts of Bray, has been the home of the Brabazon family (Earls of Meath) since 1618. The house dates from this period, but in 1820 the architect Richard Morrison remodelled it, and the gardens have been enhanced and added to over the years. In 1852 an orangery was added, which contains a collection of statues, mainly from Italy. Other attractions are the water clock, the long ponds, and the statue gallery, based on the Crystal Palace in London. Concerts and plays are held here as part of the Music in Great Houses scheme, and there is also an outdoor theatre. The house and garden are open to the public.

MOUNT USHER GARDENS, ASHFORD

Mount Usher Gardens, among of the most famous gardens in Ireland, are in the village of Ashford. In 1860 Edward Walpole saw the potential of the grounds surrounding an old corn mill in the Vartry valley. He began developing the land, where water has seldom been used to better advantage. The garden, of 20 acres (8 hectares), now contains about five thousand different types of plants and trees, including magnolias, rhododendrons, camellias, and eucalyptus. Several ornate bridges span the Vartry River, which passes through the garden. In summer there is a vast array of colour surrounding the small waterfalls, tiny streams, and overhanging trees. Mount Usher is open to the public. There is also a tea-room and craft shops.

POWERSCOURT WATERFALL

One of the most impressive features of the Powerscourt Demesne is the 351-foot (107-metre) waterfall, the highest in Ireland. The water tumbles down a cliff face and runs through the Dargle Glen, and has served as a backdrop for many photo shoots and films.

GLENDALOUGH

From the sixth century Glendalough was a place of pilgrimage. The remains of the monastic settlement and its round tower have survived centuries of conflict and the elements. The many monuments and churches spread over a two-mile radius include Teampall na Sceilge, St Kevin's Bed, St Mary's Church, Reefert Church, the round tower, the Priest's House, the cathedral, St Kevin's Church, St Kieran's Church, Trinity Church, St Saviour's Priory, and a number of crosses. Glendalough is also famed for its magnificent scenery of lakes and mountains. Glendalough Visitors' Centre, at the entrance to the valley, houses an exhibition and an audiovisual history of the area. There are regular guided tours of the religious sites, and St Kevin's Bus Service operates a service between Dublin and Glendalough. There are nine colour-marked walks around the valley.

THE MEETING OF THE WATERS

Two centuries ago the poet Thomas Moore immortalised the picturesque meeting of the Avonmore and Avonbeg Rivers, close to Avoca. The remains of the tree under which he is reputed to have written the classic song are beside the river.

NATIONAL GARDEN EXHIBITION CENTRE

The National Garden Exhibition Centre is at Kilquade, off the N11 road two miles south of the Glen of the Downs. The centre comprises nineteen gardens, creating a diversity and contrast between large and small gardens. There is also a tea-room.

THE DWYER-MCALLISTER COTTAGE

This whitewashed thatched cottage is on the Knockanarrigan–Rathdangan road in the wilds of the Glen of Imail. In 1799 it was the centre of an exchange between the insurgent leader Michael Dwyer and a force of Redcoats. While the soldiers burned the cottage, Dwyer made an amazing escape over the snow-capped mountains. In 1946 the cottage was restored as a monument to Dwyer; in 1992 it was renovated and it is now open to the public during the summer months.

BRITTAS BAY BEACH

Brittas Bay, north of Arklow, with a two-mile sandy beach sheltered by sand dunes, is one of the most popular stretches of beach on the east coast. Rare species of plant life are to be found among the dunes.

WICKLOW MOUNTAINS NATIONAL PARK

Wicklow Mountains National Park covers much of the upland of Co. Wicklow, comprising an area of approximately 75,000 acres (30,000 hectares), extending from Killakee, Co. Dublin, in the north to Lugnaquillia Mountain in the south, including large tracts of blanket bogs. Within the park are many archaeological sites, including stone circles and passage tombs dating from the Stone Age. The park serves as a protective zone for wildlife, from rare orchids to deer and the peregrine falcon.

The WICKLOW WAY

The Wicklow Way is an 81-mile (131-kilometre) signposted walking trail suitable for beginner and expert alike. In fact the walk neither starts nor finishes in Co. Wicklow: Marlay Park in Rathfarnham, Co. Dublin, is the northern starting-point, and it reaches its southernmost point in Clonegal, Co. Carlow. The idea was the brainchild of the journalist and inveterate walker J. B. Malone, who first suggested it in 1966, and it was implemented in 1978. Since then the 'walking man' symbol has become a familiar sight in the countryside; square black posts mark the course, with yellow arrowheads pointing the way. Along the route there are also map boards to assist walkers.

There are seven recommended walks, individual sections of the Wicklow Way, each with local variations for shorter routes. The walks keep mainly to the eastern flanks of the mountains and generally do not cross summits but keep to existing paths that have been traversed for thousands of years by soldiers and pilgrims, who have left few other traces of their lives. Some circular walks return to a car park or bus route. Approximately forty car parks are dotted along the trail. The longer treks, for experienced walkers, have eight An Óige hostels along the route for weary travellers.

WICKLOW GARDENS FESTIVAL

The Wicklow Gardens Festival is now established as Ireland's foremost gardens festival. While the larger gardens are open throughout the year, most of the smaller gardens open only on certain days during the festival, which is held from 1 May to 31 July. They range from seventeenth-century landscaped gardens to the recently created smaller cottage gardens. Plants on display vary from great trees and shrubs to herbaceous plants and the smallest alpine flowers.

SPORT

The TOUR DE FRANCE

In 1998 Co. Wicklow was under the international spotlight when 96 miles of the 112-mile stage of the Tour de France were routed through the county, the first time the Tour de France was held outside the continent of Europe. This followed Stephen Roche's victory in the race in 1987, when he became the first Irish cyclist to win. The race began in Dublin and proceeded through the mountains and glens of Co. Wicklow. These roads were familiar to Stephen Roche, as he had trained there as a young cyclist before going as a professional to the Continent. Many stretches of the road network were resurfaced for the event.

In 1963 Shay Elliott became the first Irishman to wear the yellow jersey in the Tour de France. He had trained on the roads of Co. Wicklow, and a memorial has been erected to him by the Bray Wheelers Cycling Club on a stretch known as the 'Shay Elliott Mile'.

GAA

Co. Wicklow has a strong GAA tradition, dating back to the foundation of the organisation. The county grounds are in Aughrim. The county has never succeeded in reaching either a hurling or a football senior all-Ireland semi-final.

The Gaelic Athletic Association was founded in Thurles in November 1884 to preserve and cultivate native games. The first game under GAA rules to be played in Co. Wicklow was in the following October, between Ashford and Dalkey. In 1885 the first Co. Wicklow GAA Convention was held. When Bray Emmets were founded the same year, the players were kept under surveillance by order of Dublin Castle. By 1891 the club had a membership of 275. Delgany Shamrocks were another of the earliest teams to be established in the county.

Co. Wicklow was one of twelve counties in the first all-Ireland championship. They were drawn against Clare. Though the county has not had a memorable record at senior level, the minors and under-21 football teams have won many victories. In 1936 Wicklow won an all-Ireland junior football title, and in 1989 Baltinglass won the all-Ireland club championship. In 1992 Wicklow won the all-Ireland B championship. In 1961 Hugh Byrne of Wicklow became president of the GAA, followed in 1994 by Jack Boothman.

BRAY WANDERERS

Bray Wanderers are the only League of Ireland (soccer) team in Co. Wicklow. They have had an erratic history, being relegated and promoted to the Premier Division on a number of occasions. Their home grounds are the Carlisle Grounds, Bray, opened in September 1862 and named after the Lord Lieutenant, Lord Carlisle.

In 1922 a dispute arose in a local GAA team, St Kevin's, which resulted in some members leaving the association and forming a soccer team, which they named Bray Wanderers. Most of the members and players were from the locality, but as the club's reputation grew they recruited from a wider area. In the mid-1930s the team went into a decline, partly because of the insecurity of tenure of their grounds. This was resolved, and the team re-formed in 1942. Shortly afterwards they moved into Division 2. In 1963 the team was again in decline, and they changed their name to the Bray Unknowns; in an effort to return to the senior league they reverted to their original name in 1973. The team was twice League of Ireland championship winner, in 1985/86 and 1995/96. In 1990 they won the most treasured trophy, the FAI Senior Cup.

One player who distinguished himself with Bray Wanderers was their goalkeeper, Alan Kelly, who joined them in 1954 and was capped forty-seven times for Ireland. His son, also Alan Kelly, was to follow in this tradition and became goalkeeper for Sheffield United. He received his first cap for Ireland in 1993, under Jack Charlton.

In September 1997 the film director Neil Jordan used the Carlisle Grounds to re-create the Bloody Sunday massacre of November 1920 (when Black and Tans shot dead several players and spectators) for his film *Michael Collins.* The grounds have recently undergone renovation, with new facilities for players and spectators alike.

BRAY WHEELERS

In 1949 Bray Wheelers Cycle Club was founded. Some of its members have won national competitions and have represented the country at the Olympic Games in Rome in 1960, in Mexico in 1968, and in Munich in 1972.

ATHLETICS

In 1956, at the Melbourne Olympic Games, 21-year-old Ronnie Delany won the gold medal in the 1,500 metres. Delany was born in Arklow on 6 March 1935. He graduated from Villanova University, Pennsylvania, with a B.Sc., having been coached by Jim (Jumbo) Elliott and at 18 he reached the European Championship 1,500 metres final in 1954. He was undefeated indoors in the USA throughout a career of 40 races, including 34 at the mile. He became the seventh man to break the four-minute barrier for the mile.

GOLF

Co. Wicklow has a selection of golf courses, from driving-ranges and pitch-and-putt to nine-hole and eighteen-hole courses; the most popular clubs in the county include Delgany, Druid's Glen, Blainroe, Woodbrook, Greystones, Bray, Powerscourt, Rathsallagh, and Coolattin. The Druid's Glen course was chosen in consecutive years for the Irish Open Golf Championship in 1996 and 1997.

WATER SPORTS

Co. Wicklow, with its sea coast and many rivers and lakes, has an abundance of water sports, including sailing, canoeing, rowing, swimming, windsurfing, and river, lake, and shore fishing. Cruises on the Blessington lakes are available on the *Blessington,* a luxury 72-seat cruiser.

FISHING

In 1995 the International Sea Fishing Championship was held in Wicklow. The coastline from Bray to Arklow offers many suitable sites for shore angling.

YACHT CLUBS

On a number of occasions Wicklow Head has been the starting-point for the Round Ireland Yacht Race. Annual regattas are also held in Wicklow and Bray and attract teams from along the east coast.

SWIMMING

The swimming champion Gary O'Toole was born in Bray. He became a member of Bray Cove and Trojan Swimming Clubs and made his swimming debut at sixteen. He attended the European Swimming Championships in Bonn and became the first Irish swimmer to win a medal at that level. In 1990 he set seven Irish swimming records. In 1991 he won the Gold Medal in the 200-metre breast stroke at the World Student Games, and in 1992 he represented Ireland at the Barcelona Olympics in his speciality event, the 200 metres breast stroke.

HANDBALL

John Lawlor, who was to gain an international reputation as a handballer, was born in Pennsylvania in 1860. His family returned to Ireland, and he spent his childhood in Kiltegan, Co. Wicklow. He won the Irish Professional Handball Championship title for four consecutive years, 1885–88. He also won the Handball Championship of the World. In 1923 he became the first president of the Irish Amateur Handball Association.

RACING

Co. Wicklow has a long tradition of equine sports and is dotted with stud farms and pony-trekking centres. In March 1958 Mr What, owned by David Coughlan of King Edward Road, Bray, won the Aintree Grand National.

BLOTS ON *The* LANDSCAPE

Over the past decade a number of developments have cast a pall over the environment of Co. Wicklow. One has been the problem of indiscriminate illegal dumping in lanes and fields, including household refuse, builder's rubble, and hospital waste. A more obvious eyesore has been the widespread erection of unsightly electricity pylons stretching across valleys and mountains. The opening of a McDonald's fast-food outlet in the 120-year-old town hall in Bray caused protests and a huge amount of controversy.

LOCAL MEDIA

East Coast Radio, broadcasting on 94.9, 96.2, 102.9, and 104.4 FM, is a popular local radio station that provides music, magazine, and sports programmes and an entertainment guide. The *Wicklow People* and *Bray People* and their local editions are part of the Independent group of newspapers, while the *Wicklow Times* is delivered free to every house in the district.

PLACES OF INTEREST

Wicklow Historic Jail
Cliff walk, Bray to Greystones
Franciscan Abbey, Wicklow
Lake drive, Lacken
Black Castle, Wicklow
Clara Vale (scenic)
Dwyer's Cottage, Glen of Imail
Woodenbridge (scenic)
St Kevin's Bed, Glendalough
Parnell Memorial Park, Rathdrum
Monastic settlement, Glendalough
Burial mound, Baltinglass
Glendalough Lakes
Glenroe Open Farm, Kilcoole
National Garden Exhibition Centre, Kilquade
Maritime Museum, Arklow
Heritage Centre, Bray
Sea Life, Bray
Hangman Gallery, Bray
Signal Arts Gallery, Bray
German War Cemetery, Glencree
Glenmacnass Waterfall
Meeting of the Waters, Avoca
Avoca Handweavers, Avoca and Kilmacanogue
Motte stone, Avoca
Ashford cattle mart (Monday)
Ballinastoe Pottery, Roundwood

Wild Irish Crafts, Shillelagh
Derrylossary Church, Callary

CALENDAR OF EVENTS

Bray One-Act Drama Festival, Bray (January)
Rathdrum Easter Walking Festival (April)
Taste of Wicklow Festival (May)
Wicklow Mountains Walking Festival (May)
County Wicklow Garden Festival (May)
Moore's Melody Fair, Avoca (May)
Glen of Imail Deer Fair (June)
Dunlavin Festival of Arts (June)
Bray Seaside Festival (July)
Synge Summer School, Rathdrum (July)
Arklow Gardens of Ireland Festival (July)
Greystones Arts Festival (August)
Wicklow Regatta Festival (August)
Arklow Maritime Festival (August)
County Agricultural Show, Tinahely (August)
Parnell Summer School, Rathdrum (August)
Enniskerry Victorian Festival (September)
Heritage Day, guided historical walks (September)
ICA Festival of One-Act Plays, Glenealy (October)
Oscar Wilde Autumn School, Bray (October)

HOUSES AND GARDENS

Avondale House and Forest Park, Rathdrum
Mount Usher Gardens, Ashford
Powerscourt Gardens and Waterfall, Enniskerry
Russborough House and Gardens, Blessington
Kilruddery House and Gardens, Bray
Kilmacurragh House and Gardens, Kilbride
Kilmurray Grove Gardens, Kilmacanogue
Greenan Farm Museum and Maze, Rathdrum
National Gardens Exhibition Centre, Kilpedder
Hillview Gardens, Kiltegan
Rathsallagh House, Dunlavin

TOURIST OFFICES

Arklow
Ashford
Blessington
Bray
Glendalough
Laragh
Rathdrum
Wicklow

FOREST TRAILS

Ballinadunshoge, near Rathdrum
Ballinastoe Wood, south of Enniskerry
Ballygannon, Rathdrum
Barravore Wood, Laragh
Crone Wood, Enniskerry
Devil's Glen, Ashford
Djouce Wood, near Enniskerry
Glenart, Arklow
Hollywood Wood
Kilmacurragh Arboretum
Kindlestown Wood, Delgany
Knocksink Wood, Enniskerry
Lugnagroagh, Blessington
Trooperstown Wood, Laragh
Wicklow National Park
Wicklow Way

HOSTELS

Aughavanagh
Ballinclea
Baltyboys, Blessington
Glendalough
Glenmalure
Knockree-Enniskerry
Tiglin, Ashford

ACTIVITIES

Annamoe Trout Farm, Annamoe
Ballinacree Open Farm, Enniskerry
Bel-Air Riding School, Ashford
Blessington Lakes Leisure Pursuits Centre, Blessington
Bray International Leisure Bowl, Bray
Bray Sailing Club
Clara Lara Fun Park
Devil's Glen Forest and Equestrian Centre
Laragh Trekking Centre, Laragh
Shillelagh Pony Trekking, Shillelagh
Tiglin Adventure Centre, Ashford
Wicklow Sailing Club

Appendix 1
CENSUS OF POPULATION

IN THE CENSUS OF 1996 the population of Co. Wicklow exceeded 100,000 for the first time since 1841. An increase of 5,000 over the previous five years brought the total to 102,683; this made Co. Wicklow the twelfth most populous county in the country. The census of 2002 recorded an increase of 12 per cent, bringing the total to 114,719.

There has been rapid growth in population and development in the larger towns, which have largely become dormitory towns; this is particularly true of Blessington, Wicklow, Greystones, and Bray. Surprisingly, between 1996 and 2002 the population of Bray rose only from 25,252 to 26,215. In many households, both adults commuted to and from Dublin, adding to the traffic congestion. There has been large-scale construction of apartments and town houses in Bray in particular to accommodate these commuters. On the other hand there has been a decline in the population of rural Co. Wicklow. In rural areas women outnumber men, while the opposite is true for the urban areas.

CO. WICKLOW

1841	126,143
1851	98,979
1861	86,479
1871	78,697
1881	70,386
1891	62,136
1901	60,824
1911	60,711
1926	57,591
1936	58,569
1946	60,451
1951	62,590
1961	58,473
1971	66,295
1981	87,449
1991	97,265
2002	114,719

ELECTORAL DISTRICTS

BALTINGLASS

1971	8,710
1979	10,454
1981	10,741
1986	11,902
1991	11,967
1996	12,749
2002	14,715

BRAY

1971	15,537
1979	21,773
1981	22,853
1986	24,686
1991	25,096
1996	25,252
2002	26,216

RATHDOWN

1971	7,895
1979	11,258
1981	11,874
1986	13,613
1991	15,093
1996	16,395
2002	19,025

ARKLOW

1971	6,948
1979	8,451
1981	8,646
1986	8,388
1991	7,987
1996	8,519
2002	9,962

WICKLOW

1971	3,786
1979	4,981
1981	5,178
1986	5,304
1991	5,847
1996	6,416
2002	7,007

RATHDRUM

1971	17,398
1979	20,809
1981	21,981
1986	24,254
1991	24,865
1996	26,932
2002	31,085

SHILLELAGH

1971	6,021
1979	6,224
1981	6,176
1986	6,395
1991	6,410
1996	6,420
2002	6,708

Appendix 2 PUBLIC REPRESENTATIVES *for* CO. WICKLOW

FIRST DÁIL (DECEMBER 1918)

Robert Barton (Sinn Féin), J. R. Etchingham (Sinn Féin)

SECOND DÁIL (MAY 1921)

Art O'Connor (Sinn Féin), Domhnall Ó Buachalla (Sinn Féin), Erskine Childers (Sinn Féin), Robert Barton (Sinn Féin), Christopher Byrne (Cumann na nGaedheal).

THIRD DÁIL (AUGUST 1923)

Robert Barton (Sinn Féin), James Everett (Labour Party), R. Wilson (Farmers' Party), Christopher Byrne (Cumann na nGaedheal), Hugh Colohan (Labour Party).

FOURTH DÁIL (AUGUST 1923)

James Everett (Labour Party), Christopher Byrne (Cumann na nGaedheal), R. Wilson (Farmers' Party).

FIFTH DÁIL (JUNE 1927)

James Everett (Labour Party), Séamus Moore (Fianna Fáil), The O'Mahony (Cumann na nGaedheal).

SIXTH DÁIL (SEPTEMBER 1927)

James Everett (Labour Party), Séamus Moore (Fianna Fáil), The O'Mahony (Cumann na nGaedheal).

SEVENTH DÁIL (SEPTEMBER 1932)

James Everett (Labour Party), Séamus Moore (Fianna Fáil), The O'Mahony (Cumann na nGaedheal).

EIGHTH DÁIL (JANUARY 1933)

James Everett (Labour Party), Séamus Moore (Fianna Fáil), The O'Mahony (Fine Gael).

NINTH DÁIL (JULY 1937)

James Everett (Labour Party), Séamus Moore (Fianna Fáil), The O'Mahony (Fine Gael).

TENTH DÁIL (JUNE 1938)

James Everett (Labour Party), Séamus Moore (Fianna Fáil), Patrick Cogan (independent).

ELEVENTH DÁIL (JUNE 1943)

James Everett (Labour Party), Christopher Byrne (Fianna Fáil), Patrick Cogan (independent).

TWELFTH DÁIL (MAY 1944)

James Everett (Labour Party), Patrick Cogan (independent), Thomas Brennan (Fianna Fáil).

THIRTEENTH DÁIL (FEBRUARY 1948)

James Everett (Labour Party), Patrick Cogan (Farmers' Party), Thomas Brennan (Fianna Fáil).

FOURTEENTH DÁIL (MAY 1951)

James Everett (Labour Party), Patrick Cogan (Farmers' Party), Thomas Brennan (Fianna Fáil). 1953 by-election: Mark Deering (Fine Gael).

FIFTEENTH DÁIL (MAY 1954)

James Everett (Labour Party), Mark Deering (Fine Gael), Paudge Brennan (Fianna Fáil).

SIXTEENTH DÁIL (MARCH 1957)

James Everett (Labour Party), James O'Toole (Fianna Fáil), Paudge Brennan (Fianna Fáil).

SEVENTEENTH DÁIL (OCTOBER 1961)

James Everett (Labour Party), Michael J. O'Higgins (Fine Gael), Paudge Brennan (Fianna Fáil).

EIGHTEENTH DÁIL (APRIL 1965)

James Everett (Labour Party), Michael J. O'Higgins (Fine Gael), Paudge Brennan (Fianna Fáil). 1968 by-election: Godfrey Timmins (Fine Gael).

NINETEENTH DÁIL (JUNE 1969)

Liam Kavanagh (Labour Party), Paudge Brennan (Fianna Fáil), Godfrey Timmins (Fine Gael).

TWENTIETH DÁIL (FEBRUARY 1973)

Liam Kavanagh (Labour Party), Godfrey Timmins (Fine Gael), Ciarán Murphy (Fianna Fáil).

TWENTY-FIRST DÁIL (JUNE 1977)

Liam Kavanagh (Labour Party), Godfrey Timmins (Fine Gael), Ciarán Murphy (Fianna Fáil).

TWENTY-SECOND DÁIL (JUNE 1981)

Liam Kavanagh (Labour Party), Godfrey Timmins (Fine Gael), Ciarán Murphy (Fianna Fáil), Paudge Brennan (Fianna Fáil).

TWENTY-THIRD DÁIL (FEBRUARY 1982)

Liam Kavanagh (Labour Party), Godfrey Timmins (Fine Gael), Ciarán Murphy (Fianna Fáil), Gemma Hussey (Fine Gael).

TWENTY-FOURTH DÁIL (NOVEMBER 1982)

Liam Kavanagh (Labour Party), Godfrey Timmins (Fine Gael), Paudge Brennan (Fianna Fáil), Gemma Hussey (Fine Gael).

TWENTY-FIFTH DÁIL (FEBRUARY 1987)

Dick Roche (Fianna Fáil), Joe Jacob (Fianna Fáil), Liam Kavanagh (Labour Party), Gemma Hussey (Fine Gael).

TWENTY-SIXTH DÁIL (JUNE 1989)

Dick Roche (Fianna Fáil), Joe Jacob (Fianna Fáil), Liam Kavanagh (Labour Party), Godfrey Timmins (Fine Gael).

TWENTY-SEVENTH DÁIL (DECEMBER 1992)

Joe Jacob (Fianna Fáil), Liam Kavanagh (Labour Party), Johnny Fox (independent), Liz McManus (Democratic Left), Godfrey Timmins (Fine Gael). 1995 by-election: Mildred Fox (independent).

TWENTY-EIGHTH DÁIL (JUNE 1997)

Joe Jacob (Fianna Fáil), Dick Roche (Fianna Fáil), Liz McManus (Democratic Left), Billy Timmins (Fine Gael), Mildred Fox (independent).

TWENTY-NINTH DÁIL (MAY 2002)

Joe Jacob (Fianna Fáil), Dick Roche (Fianna Fáil), Liz McManus (Labour Party), Billy Timmins (Fine Gael), Mildred Fox (independent).

WOMEN POLITICIANS

It was sixty-four years after the first Dáil Éireann that the first woman deputy was elected in Co. Wicklow. The Fine Gael candidate, Gemma Hussey, was elected to the twenty-third Dáil in February 1982; she was to be re-elected in 1982 and 1987. During this period Fine Gael had two TDs in Co. Wicklow, Gemma Hussey and Godfrey Timmins. Hussey was to serve as Minister for Education, Social Welfare, and Labour.

The next woman to be elected in the county was Liz McManus for Democratic Left in December 1992. Later a member of the Labour Party, she became Minister of State at the Department of the Environment, 1994–97.

The third woman elected was the independent Mildred Fox, who won a by-election in June 1995 caused by the death of her father, the sitting TD, Johnny Fox. She was the youngest member of the 27th Dáil and the only female independent deputy in the 27th and 28th Dáil. In 1997 McManus and Fox were re-elected, and Fox became one of the four independent TDs who supported the coalition Government of Fianna Fáil and the Progressive Democrats. In 2002 both McManus and Fox were re-elected.

In 1994 the Green Party candidate, Nuala Ahern, was elected as a Member of the European Parliament (MEP) for Leinster.

SELECT BIBLIOGRAPHY

Annals of the Kingdom of Ireland, The Four Masters, translated by John O'Donovan, Dublin, 1860.
Arklow Historical Society Journal, 1984.
Beckett, J.C., and James Camlin, *A Short History of Ireland,* London: Hutchinson, 1973.
Boylan, Henry, *A Dictionary of Irish Biography,* Dublin: Gill and Macmillan, 1988.
Bray Journal 1985, Cualann Historical Society, 1985.
Brien, Christopher, *In the Lands of Brien,* Bray: privately published, 1984.
Brophy, Jim, *By the Banks of the Dargle,* Bray Emmets, 1985.
Brophy, Jim, *The Leather Echo,* Wicklow GAA, 1984.
Brophy, Jim, and Arthur Flynn, *The Book of Wicklow,* Bray: Kestrel Books, 1991.
Bye-laws of Bray Township Commissioners, 1897.
Charlesworth, J.K., *Historical Geology of Ireland,* London: Oliver and Boyd, 1966.
De Latocnaye, *A Frenchman's Walk Through Ireland, 1796–7,* Belfast: Blackstaff Press, 1984.
De Lion, Caoimhin, *Vale of Avoca,* Dublin: Kamac, 1967.
Dickson, Charles, *The Life of Michael Dwyer,* Dublin, 1944.
Down Survey, Sir William Petty, Irish Archaeological Society, Dublin, 1851.
Doyle, Oliver, and Stephen Hirsch, *Railways in Ireland,* Dublin, 1984.
Dublin Historical Record, Old Dublin Society, 1939.
Flynn, Arthur, *Famous Links with Bray,* Bray: Falcon Press, 1985.
Flynn, Arthur, *History of Bray,* Cork: Mercier Press, 1986.
Forde, Frank, *Maritime Arklow,* Dublin: Glendale Press, 1988.
For the Betterment of the People, Wicklow County Council, 1999.
Furlong, Nicky, *Dermot King of Leinster and Foreigners,* Dublin: Anvil, 1973.

Garner, William, *Bray: An Architectural Heritage*, Dublin: An Foras Forbartha, 1980.
Gaskin, J., and Patrick Traynor, *Irish Varieties*, Dublin, 1878.
Harvey, John, *Dublin – A Study in Environment*, London: Batsford, 1949.
Hogan, Robert, *The Macmillan Dictionary of Irish Literature*, London: Macmillan, 1979.
A Hundred Years of Bray and Neighbourhood by An Old Inhabitant, Dublin: Carraig Books, 1978.
Hollywood – A Wicklow Village, Hollywood History Group.
Inglis, H.D., *Journey Through Ireland*, London: Whittaker, 1834.
Jennings, Robert, *Glimpses of an Ancient Parish, Newcastle, Co. Wicklow, 1189–1989*, privately published, 1989.
Journal of the West Wicklow Historical Society, various, 1984–.
Kiggins, Thomas, *Maynooth Mission to Africa*, Dublin: Gill & Macmillan, 1991.
Lewis, Samuel, *Topographical Dictionary of Ireland*, London, 1837.
Loughrey, Frank, *Sunbeam House*, Bray: privately published, 1997.
Malone, J.B., *The Complete Wicklow Way*, Dublin: O'Brien Press, 1988.
McCarthy Hugh, *A History of Rathdrum*, privately published, n.d.
McMahon, Sean, *Rich and Rare*, Dublin: Poolbeg Press, 1999.
Moody, T.W., and F.X. Martin, *The Course of Irish History*, Cork: Mercier Press, 1967.
Mulligan, Fergus, *150 Years of the Railway*, Belfast: Appletree Press, 1983.
Murphy, Denis, *Cromwell in Ireland*, Dublin: M.H. Gill & Son, 1897.
Murray, K.A., *Ireland's 1st Railway, Dublin*, 1981.
O'Sullivan, Thomas F., *The Story of the GAA*, Dublin: privately published, 1961.
O'Toole, Rev. P.L., *O'Toole's and Other Leinster Septs*, privately published, n.d.
Pakenham, Thomas, *The Year of Liberty*, London: Weidenfeld & Nicolson, 1997.
Power, P.J., *The Pocket Guide to South-East Wicklow*, 1989.
Price, Liam, *The Place Names of County Wicklow*, 7 vols, Dublin: Institute for Advanced Studies, 1957.
Rees, Jim, and Liam Charlton, *Arklow – Last Stronghold of Sail*, Dublin, 1985.
Scott, George Digby, *The Stones of Bray*, Bray: Cualann Publications, 1984.
Thom's Irish Who's Who, Dublin, 1923.
Walsh, Caroline, *The Homes of Irish Writers*, Dublin: Anvil Books, 1982.
West Wicklow, A Guide, Dublin, 1971.
Wicklow Historical Society Journal, various, 1984–.

Burke's Peerage
Bray People
Freeman's Journal
Index to References in County Wicklow
Irish Railway Record Society
Irish Times
Ireland's Own
Journals, Newspapers, and Dictionaries
Saunder's Newsletter
Thom's Directory
Wicklow People

INDEX